THE GUIDE TO

Good Eating
In St. Louis

A Treasury of Area Bakeries, Restaurants,
Specialty Food Shops, and Farms

Susan Taylor

Cover design and illustrations by
Laurie Eisenbach-Bush

Fifth Sin Press

The Guide to Good Eating in St. Louis

Fifth Sin Press
P.O. Box 170143
St. Louis, MO 63117

Cover design and illustrations by Laurie Eisenbach-Bush
Edited by E. Bumas

Library of Congress Cataloging-in-Publication Number: 94-94294
ISBN 0-9640998-3-7

Publisher's Cataloging-in-Publication Data
Taylor, Susan. The guide to good eating in St. Louis
1. Restaurants, lunchrooms, etc.—Missouri—St. Louis region—Guide-books. 2. Marketing (Home economics)—Missouri—St. Louis region—Guide-books. 3. Farmers' markets—Missouri—St. Louis region—Guide-books.
Includes Index

Manufactured in the United States of America
Printed on acid-free recycled paper

To "my boys," Stephen and Daniel, with love.

Introduction

Food provides us with nourishment, ritual, and cultural identity. Food is a cord that connects us to the rhythm of the earth and to our particular heritages. Yet, in breaking bread with different people, we can transcend cultural barriers. Food allows us to blend and expand our experience and to maintain the uniqueness of our own culture. Here in St. Louis, where the city meets some of the world's richest farmland, where numerous cultures come together, and where local chefs, bakers, shopkeepers, and farmers are exploring and expanding culinary boundaries, we are in the midst of an explosion of culinary creativity. This book, with more than 150 places to buy an immense variety of food, is a recognition and celebration of that creativity.

I'm a newcomer to St. Louis—a city girl who has returned to urban life after an eight-year stop in a mid-sized town in a rural area. No, St. Louis isn't my native Detroit and Chicago, but life in all big cities has a style and cadence that transcends geography and allows me to be at home as I explore the particular rhythms of my adopted city. And what better way is there to begin to draw out the unique personality of St. Louis than by digging into its culinary bounty?

I have found passion in the culinary life of the metro area and in the rich farmland that surrounds and sustains St. Louis. I see it in the chefs of the recently founded "St. Louis Friends of James Beard," a society that gathers four times a year to combine their members' creative energy in cooking sumptuous meals that expand the boundaries of our culinary experience. I see this passion in farmers who proudly rattle off the names of some of the 40 varieties of tomatoes they grow, or who plant 50 varieties of apples and hope their visitors will try them all, or who stubbornly persist in planting nectarine trees in this climate that kills more of these delicate trees than it nurtures. It is in the sausage maker who enriches this city by creating classic European sausages in his humble neighborhood shop, and in the bread bakers who are going back to the basics of bread making to give us real bread, baked the hard way. It exists in the immigrant communities of St. Louis, where people tenaciously hold on to their cultural traditions and bake Chinese mooncakes, French tarts, Lebanese walnut cookies, Italian biscotti, Danish sweet rolls, and German strudel. I see it in those newcomers who find local farmers to plant the seeds they gleaned from their native plants before immigrating. It is in those who live on the mighty rivers and remind us with their offerings of wild mushrooms or fresh "coon" that even today our food can be foraged.

In this book, you will find out where to buy hundreds of specialty foods, including foods imported from Asia, the Indian subcontinent, the Caribbean, Europe, North Africa, the Middle East, and Latin America. You will find out where to buy bagels, German rye bread, French baguettes, soft pretzels, and fresh pita, as well as homemade ice cream, fine chocolates, and sweet potato pie. If cheese is your passion, this book will tell you where to buy 200 varieties of imported cheese, as well as raw-milk cheese that you can order by mail. Kosher meat, 100 varieties of locally produced European sausages, fresh fish, and locally raised lamb are only some of the other offerings you will find.

The section on local farms will tell you where to go to find asparagus and morel mushrooms; where you can pick strawberries, raspberries, and blueberries; where to buy peaches, nectarines, pears, plums, and 60 varieties of apples; where to find 40 varieties of tomatoes, and 80 varieties of fresh herbs and herb plants. These farms are all within an hour's drive from St. Louis and make a great trip into the country where you can pick berries or stock up for the winter on locally grown apples from the approximately 60 varieties available.

There are hundreds of restaurants in the St. Louis area. In this book, I describe a sampling of the best and most unusual. I looked for places that people might seek out when visiting St. Louis—restaurants that they might not find in smaller towns, or restaurants that characterize St. Louis in some way. Some of the menus may have changed by the time you visit, but I have tried to describe the restaurants' styles, so that you can make restaurant choices on the basis of style. There are undoubtedly places I have missed and others that will open, all of which I would like to cover in some future edition. I want to assure my readers that I did not accept compensation from any establishment in exchange for inclusion in this book.

This book is organized in four sections, each arranged alphabetically. The last section, Fresh from the Country, separates markets, farms in Missouri, and farms in Illinois, and lists them alphabetically. Also in this section, you will find a list of taverns that sell morel mushrooms in season, a description of 50 varieties of apples, and an assortment of local mail-order foods. A good area map is important, whether you are trying to find a farm or a shop. I tried to be helpful by giving the names of towns in which places are located. I also included ZIP codes to help you locate a general area on the map. In case you still aren't sure where a specific place is, I've provided phone numbers that you should call to ask for directions. All of these places are businesses—they want you to find them!

I have attempted to give you a general idea of the cost of eating at restaurants. Of course, prices change, but basic categories, within a dollar or two, will remain fairly stable. Restaurants that I call "inexpensive" serve entrees for less than $8.00. Those that are "moderate" are priced from $8.00 to $17.00, and "expensive" ones are these at which you can expect to pay more than $17.00. Please check the hours of a restaurant, as they do change, and except for all but the most casual restaurants, call well in advance to find out if reservations are necessary.

I am thoroughly enjoying living in St. Louis, and the conclusion of this book will not end my food explorations. I hope this book will help you discover some of the passion that goes into creating St. Louis's culinary treasures.

Susan Taylor
May, 1994

Thanks

Many people contributed to this book and I would like to thank them. Special thanks to Nancy Howard Higgins, who not only encouraged me to write this book, but also helped introduce me to St. Louis's culinary life. Thanks to Laurie Eisenbach-Bush for capturing the spirit of the book in her bold, whimsical cover design and illustrations.

Perhaps the greatest contribution I received was encouragement, and it came from many sources. Ann Laurence and Ross Richardson have been a two-person cheerleading squad; my childhood friend, Margo Green, was always available to introduce me to her town; Heidi Levin came from Chicago to take wonderfully perceptive photographs that I use to promote my books; Chef Michael Higgins shared valuable insights from the other side of the kitchen door; Karen Hewitt has been an indispensable source of publishing information.

Thanks to Tom Curran from the St. Louis County Department of Planning for help in untangling the complex web that makes up the St. Louis metropolitan area so that I could create an accurate area index. Thanks also to Brian Smart and Bil Vincent for their help with the manuscript.

I spoke to dozens of people in coffee houses, food shops, on the playground, and elsewhere, who generously shared their opinions and knowledge of the city's culinary treasures. I thank them, and I thank our old friends as well as the new friends we made who accompanied us to meals and who tolerated much probing and swapping during these meals. I want to express my gratitude to the chefs, bakers, farmers, orchardists, and shopkeepers who take enormous risks in order to expand our culinary experience.

Thanks to my son Danny for his unquenchable curiosity and his growing love of good food. Most of all, I am grateful to my husband, Stephen Spence, who trusted me to do it, and do it well.

Contents

Restaurants

Special Events

A Bite to Eat

Specialty Food Shops

Chocolates and Ice Cream

Cookware Shops

Meat and Fish Markets

Coffee Shops and Coffee Houses

Fresh from the Country

Produce Markets

Missouri Farms

Illinois Farms

THE GUIDE TO

Good Eating
In St. Louis

Bakeries

Amighetti Bakery
5141 Wilson
St. Louis 63110
(314) 776-2855
Open: Tuesdays through Saturdays,
9:00 AM–8:00 PM (Saturday 7:30 AM–5:30 PM)

When shopping on the Hill stop at Amighetti's for a loaf of Italian bread. Crisp and crunchy on the outside and light, yet moist and flavorful on the inside, this is the best Italian loaf on the Hill.

The Bagel Factory
11256 Olive St. Rd.
Creve Coeur 63141
(314) 432-3583
Open: Weekdays, 7:00 AM–6:30 PM,
Saturday 7:00 AM–5:00 PM, Sunday 8:00 AM–4:00 PM

The Bagel Factory has great bagels. These are not the soft, airy roll-with-a-hole-in-the-middle-type bagels. These are the chewy on the inside, with crispy toppings on the outside, and flavorful-through-and-through-type of bagel. On weekends there's a good chance of getting your bagels hot from the oven. If you do, close the windows before driving off and savor the smell of fresh bread mingled with the enticing scents of onions and garlic. You will likely be overcome by the smell, so be sure you've put the bagels on the front seat. Reaching around to the back seat to break off a piece can be dangerous!

Made the old fashioned way with malt instead of sugar and a dunking in boiling water before baking, these large bagels come in two dozen or so varieties. The onion bagels have a coating of crunchy onions, the garlic ones have lots of aromatic garlic, the salt bagels are usually not too salty, and the deluxe combo bagel combines onion, poppy seed, sesame, salt, and cornmeal for a great flavor as well as crunch. Other flavors include egg, Russian rye, oat bran, tzitzle (corn meal topping), sesame seed, pumpernickel, and specialty flavors such as pizza and vegetable. For those who like sweet bagels, the cinnamon raisin bagels are not too sweet and have a good cinnamon flavor. Some of the other sweet flavors, such as blueberry, are best left to muffins. The Bagel Factory bakes very good bialies, a lighter version of a bagel, with a crisp crust and a crater of soft sweet onions in the center.

Bar Italia Bakery
4656 Maryland
St. Louis 63108
(314) 361-7010 or 535-5160
Open: By appointment

Marcia Sindel is the very talented baker for Bar Italia, the wonderful restaurant in the Central West End. You can buy her marvelous pastries at Bar Italia, or special order them through the restaurant or directly from her. Some of her delectable creations are not on the Bar Italia menu, but you can call her for a copy of her menu. Marcia also provides a unique service: she will help you reproduce a family heirloom cake, an historical recipe, or any dream cake that you may wish to create. She once reproduced a Mexican cake recipe that took six tries!

Many of her pastries are Italian style, with very pure flavors. Try the mini fruit tarts: the crusts on these morsels are rich and tender, and the lemon filling is intense, creamy, and has just the right amount of sugar. They come in lime and raspberry and whatever other fruit is seasonal and good. Her biscotti are very flavorful and traditionally hard. They come in almond, chocolate almond, and combined. In the style of Italy, you will find tortas made with hazelnuts, almonds, fruits, and chocolate. A simple pastry made with figs and pine nuts in a lattice crust is unique and delicious. The torta gianduia uses the classic combination of chocolate and hazelnuts in a flourless cake of ground hazelnuts glazed with chocolate. A new creation, torta de Kevin, is a chocolate lover's fantasy: moist chocolate buttermilk sponge with both dark chocolate mousse and chocolate brandy flavored mousse. Marcia bakes a Tuscan cream cake with zabaglione (the Marsala wine, egg yolk custard, and sugar custard), sponge cake, and crystallized almonds. Other fascinating creations include gingered pear pie, sweet potato cake, coconut cake, cranberry upside-down cake, and *crostada de pêche et frambois*, a lattice crusted pastry filled with peaches and raspberries. Marcia also makes wedding cakes and deep-dish savory pies for special order, and will deliver.

Basically Bagels
32 N. Euclid
St. Louis 63108
(314) 454-3003
Open: Weekdays, 6:00 AM–7:00 PM,
weekends 7:00 AM–4:00 PM

Basically Bagels bakes very good crisp-on-the-outside, chewy-on-the-inside bagels. They come with traditional coatings such as poppy seed, onion, garlic, salt, tzitzle, sesame seed, and for those who can't decide, everything. Also available are pumpernickel bagels, bialies, and bagels with cinnamon and raisins, wheat and bran, and blueberries. You can sit and read your newspaper while you enjoy a fresh bagel with one of the bakery's tasty spreads such as olive-pimento, chive, nova lox, or artichoke Parmesan. There are also fresh muffins and deli sandwiches to eat in or to go.

Companion Baking Co.
4555 Gustine Ave.
St. Louis 63116
(314) 352-4770
Open: Monday through Saturday, 7:30 AM–noon

In late 1993, Companion Baking Co. arrived on the St. Louis bread baking scene with outstanding hand crafted breads. Companion breads elevate the ordinary to the extraordinary with unique recipes and a reverence for the process of baking bread.

For the bakers, the process of creating the exquisite loaves is a celebration of the changing and unpredictable world of nature. And in eating these hand crafted works of art, we celebrate our connection to people through all time who learned how to work with basic ingredients, and to trust the invisible—wild yeast, the seasons, and time—to create nourishment.

All of the breads baked at Companion have a distinct character, and all are delicious. The *pain au levain* is a round sourdough bread with a complex fruity undertone, a crisp crust, and a moist hearty texture. It takes 50 hours to produce this bread, from building the starter to taking it out of the oven. *Pane al pomodoro* has sun-dried tomatoes, fresh garlic, olive oil, and fresh basil, added to sourdough for a rich dressed-up loaf. Bread of the country is a wonderfully hearty round loaf with a thick chewy crust and a dense interior containing unbleached white, stoneground whole wheat, and cracked wheat flours. Another version of this country bread is the five-grain hearth bread, a distinctively American variation that adds the flavors and textures of rolled oats, sunflower seeds, barley, polenta, and millet. Bread of Beauclaire is an elegant, plump, long loaf made with unbleached white flour. It has a lighter, finer texture and a softer, thinner crust. Long, skinny baguettes have crisp crust and a moist interior in a simple classic bread. The flatbread called *fougasse* gives reason to rejoice. This tree or ladder-shaped loaf is redolent with the herbs of Provence—tarragon, chervil, savory, sage, marjoram, thyme, basil, and lavender—and the earthy tang of olive oil. Cheese and sun-dried tomatoes complement the flavor of small round versions of this flatbread. And if choosing among these breads isn't hard enough, we are faced with the additional choice of buying peasant bread with figs and pine nuts. This superlative loaf dates back to the middle ages and the peasant custom of sprucing up holiday breads with sweet figs and earthy pine nuts.

As this young bakery grows, so will the line of breads. Although the bakery is in an industrial area of the city, you can also purchase your loaves at various other locations. Look for the wooden stand that artfully displays these beautiful loaves at

Brandt's, Gourmet to Go (Ladue), Protzel's Deli, the Smoke House, the Cheese Place, and Ladue Market.

Cravings Gourmet Desserts
8149 Big Bend
Webster Groves 63119
(314) 961-3534
Open: Monday through Saturday, 9:00 AM–6:00 PM
(Friday and Saturday until 11:00 PM)

Cravings is one of the new generation of bakeries that is creating outstanding pastries. You will find a selection of pastries at the new bakery and restaurant, or you can special order your dessert from an extensive list. Although many of the flavors you find at the shop are clearly influenced by European classics, Cravings has evolved its own unique style. Fresh seasonal fruit plays an important role in this style. Look for a lime-custard tart topped with blueberries in June, blackberry or apricot tarts in June or July, and cheese and dried-plum bars in the fall. Cravings makes sublime chocolate creations. Try the classic European hazelnut chocolate torte, made with hazelnut sponge cake (*génoise*), delicate chocolate mousse or whipped cream, and rich chocolate ganache. Cravings's version is stacked in a dramatic three-layer torte. Or how about chocolate cranberry cake? This fudgy cake has finely chopped cranberries that add a unique tartness and moisture. There is also chocolate mousse cake, white satin tart with raspberry puree and white chocolate mousse, and French chocolate cake with ground almonds and rum. Citrus pound cake is a dense, finely textured buttery cake flavored with fresh citrus rind and almond paste and topped in a wonderful light buttercream. Coconut roulade, rolled cake with chewy coconut, and a touch of rum in the cream filling, is simply delicious.

Those who enjoy fluffy cream-filled pastries will like the fruit cream tarts such as the raspberry one made with a crisp buttery crust and fresh raspberry cream. Cravings has good scones which are not sweet, but are rich with cream and butter. Their cookies are different from the old standards. A monster cookie—Cravings's answer to the classic chocolate chip cookie—is large with marbled chocolate and walnuts. Crisp, thin shrewsberry biscuits are a buttery treat. Coffee crisps are rich with coffee and butter. The hazelnut sandwich cookies have a chocolate center. Tea cakes, bars, miniatures, and wedding cakes are all available at this wonderful pastry shop.

The Daily Bread (formerly Nuz Pudz)
8600 Olive St. Rd.
University City 63132
(314) 997-0015
Open: Monday through Saturday,
7:00 AM–6:30 PM (Saturday until 4:30)

The Daily Bread bakes some very good and unique breads, as well as cookies, muffins, pastries, and rolls. This bakery is also a delicatessen that serves interesting fresh soups and sandwiches for lunch and take out, and breakfasts featuring muffins, croissants, and Danish. Some of the best breads at the bakery include straun, a slightly sweet bread made from corn, wheat, oats, and brown rice with a wonderful crunchy crust flavored with an abundance of poppy seeds; a bread bearing the familiar name "focaccia" that is, in fact, a totally unique crispy crusted loaf redolent with the flavors of sweet basil and garlic; ninegrain, a light oat-topped loaf with a flavorful soft interior and crunchy crust that is perfect for healthful lunch-box sandwiches; and rosemary-olive oil bread, which has just the right amount of easily overpowering rosemary. The wheat-walnut bread has a nice nutty flavor, and the cinnamon-raisin-walnut bread is sweet and full bodied. The French bread has a crisp crust and a dense interior, and the sourdough has a light sourdough flavor and a chewy interior. The pumpernickel, though, is disappointing. Good croissants at Daily Bread are large and flaky. A sweet Danish-style cheese pastry has a sweet tender pastry and a light-but-rich cream cheese filling. The cherry pastry needs more cherries. The bakery has a good selection of large cookies, some of which are good. Try the mountain cookie with chewy coconut, oatmeal, chocolate, and nuts.

Donut Drive In
6525 Chippewa (at Watson)
St. Louis 63139
(314) 645-7714
Open: Daily, 5:00 AM–midnight
(Monday until 11:00 AM, and weekends until 1:00 AM)
Another location at: 5936 Southwest (314) 647-0373

You can start your day with fresh and tasty donuts from the Donut Drive In. Try the glazed old-fashioned which is plump, dense, and flavorful, or the cinnamon twist, with cinnamon mixed throughout the dough, which is tender and light. Both have light glazes. The French donuts are light and eggy tasting, the long johns are good, and the jelly donut has lots of runny raspberry jelly. The pudding fillings used in the cream-style donuts are not dairy products.

Giegerich Pretzel Co.
2826 S. Jefferson
St. Louis 63118
(314) 664-5802
Open: Tuesday through Sunday, 6:00 AM–2:00 PM

Giegerich soft pretzels are no nonsense pretzels—a little heavier, a little saltier, and a lot less expensive than the trendier competition. At this shop, also called the thrift store, you can buy three types of pretzels: stick, round, and caraway. All are tasty, and the caraway, which are short sticks, make a nice variation. The owners offer tours of the pretzel baking operation to school children, but you must make special arrangements.

Great Harvest Bread Co.
8809 Ladue Road
(314) 721-5300
Ladue 63124
Open: Monday through Saturday,
7:00 AM–6:00 PM (Saturday until 4:30 PM)
Other locations in: Kirkwood and Chesterfield

The Great Harvest Bread Company looks like a throwback to the 1960s with its emphasis on whole grain products. But the heavy, teeth cracking breads of the sixties are only distant forerunners to the products baked here. Great Harvest proves that eating good bread can, indeed, be good for you. The breads are made with Montana wheat that is milled every day on the premises, and are sweetened with either honey or molasses. All of the whole wheat breads are full-bodied and flavorful and make the kind of peanut butter and jelly sandwich you'll be proud to send in your child's school lunch box. The sunflower honey whole wheat is a nice change with its distinctive flavor of sunflower seeds and added texture. The moist raisin-walnut-cinnamon loaf is tasty and sweet, and fresh walnut chunks add a toasted nutty flavor as well as a welcome crunch. Unfortunately, other breads in the shop fall short of their promise. Sometimes the onion-rye-dill bread offers a nice savory flavor in a lighter bread. Other times it has too much herb and onion and tastes too strong. The Swedish rye is too sweet, and the pizza bread has a too intense Italian seasoning flavor. Other specialty breads such as jalapeño cornbread, date nut spice, oatmeal poppy seed, and basil Parmesan bread are available, though not every day. The bakery bakes giant muffins and good giant cookies made with real butter. The chocolate chip walnut cookies are made with whole wheat flower and oatmeal, and the peanut butter chocolate chip cookies are chewy and full of peanut flavor.

Great Harvest always has samples available of its daily breads and cookies, so you can be sure not to go wrong in your selection. You can find this bread at various grocery stores and shops around town, but if you buy it at the bakery, you can be sure of getting a product that has been baked the same day.

Gus' Pretzel Shop
1820 Arsenal
St. Louis 63118
(314) 664-4010
Open: Tuesday through Sunday,
7:00 AM–4:00 PM (Sunday until 2:00 PM)

In the shadow of the Anheuser-Busch brewery sits Gus's, a small shop that has been turning out hand-twisted soft pretzels since 1920. But Gus's has changed with the times, and while the large soft pretzels remain excellent with their soft chewy centers, and crunchy not-too-salty exteriors, a few twists have been added to the original pretzel. The most innovative is the pretzel sandwich. Stuffed with either bratwurst or salsiccia sausage and wrapped in a pretzel stick, it is baked to a glossy golden brown. This combination really works; the salsiccia is juicy and just spicy enough, and the pretzel is crunchy on the outside and soft on the inside. At Gus's you can watch the bakers twist the dough into pretzel shapes, dunk them in their water bath, and sprinkle them with salt before baking them. You can special order party pretzels, buy them frozen to bake at home, or just take home a bag of twists and sticks for snacks.

Hank's Cheesecakes
1063 South Big Bend
Richmond Heights 63117
(314) 781-0300
Open: Tuesday through Saturday,
9:00 AM–6:00 PM (Saturday 10:00 AM–5:00 PM)

Hank's cheesecakes are creamy and delicious. Hank's gives you some three dozen flavors from which to choose and uses good quality ingredients that give each cake a distinctive flavor. The cakes are decorated simply and elegantly. They come in various sizes of round or heart-shaped. Some of the most interesting flavors are the savory cakes which come in basil pesto, herb and blue cheese, smoked salmon, and spinach and sun-dried tomato. Savory cakes have breadcrumb and herb crusts. Dessert cakes come in a variety of flavors such as butter orange, double chocolate, white chocolate raspberry, eggnog, turtle, black forest, and mocha macadamia. They bake bite-size miniatures in both sweet and savory flavors, which make nice gifts.

Hooper's Bakery
4127 Shreve Ave.
St. Louis 63115
(314) 383-7058
Open: Wednesday through Saturday,
7:00 AM–5:00 PM

Hooper's is a neighborhood bakery that has been in business for more than 40 years. The bakery specializes in small pies that are the perfect size for one person. Try the sweet potato pie with its creamy, spicy, filling and flaky crust. Peach is another good choice. For a hard-to-find treat, buy a chunk of puddin' cake. This moist, dense, spice cake is good on its own or you can try pairing it with your own rich whiskey sauce.

International Food and Bakery and Cafeteria Almadenah
3586 Adie Rd.
St. Ann 63074
(314) 298-8586
Open: Daily, 10:00 AM–9:00 PM
(Sunday 11:00 AM–6:00 PM)

Middle easterners looking for the comfort found in native food and those of us who love the authentic flavors of the middle east will love this multi-functional bakery, specialty food shop, and restaurant. The bakery produces a large variety of outstanding baked goods from perfectly fresh, tender pita bread to the pastries that we associate with the Middle East and Greece.

Wonderful baklava is made with cashews and is not over saturated with syrup. Large S-shaped butter cookies are tender and delicious. Walnut cookies, some of which are filled with dates, are crunchy and rich and have the delicate spicing of the middle east. Birds nests, made with crisp layers of phyllo dough, and shredded wheat pastries are both filled with pistachio nuts. The shop has a large selection of middle-eastern foods including teas, nuts, dried fruits, olives, halvah, tahini, grape leaves, spices, butter ghee, pickled vegetables, honey, syrup, and oils. There is a bulk section that features spices, seeds, nuts, beans, and lentils. A deli section stocks an unusual selection of cheeses, including domestic and imported cow's-milk, goat's-milk, and sheep's-milk cheeses, spiced olives, turnip pickles, and homemade yogurt.

A small restaurant serves middle eastern specialties from a menu and from a blackboard on which daily specials are written in Arabic. The *shawerma* is similar to a gyro sandwich but far superior. Made with lamb that is stacked and roasted on a vertical rotisserie and sliced thin, then piled into a split fresh pita with tomatoes, spiced onions, a slice of imported pickle, and a smooth tahini-based sauce, this spicy sandwich is wonderful. Also available are hummus (a chickpea-tahini dip), baba ghanoush (an eggplant-tahini dip), falafel (deep fried balls of ground spiced chickpeas), meat pies, spinach pies, and kibbe (beef, bulgar, onion, and pinenut patties) served either raw or cooked. For a full hot meal, ask about the daily specials.

La Bonne Bouchée Café and Bakery
12344 Olive St. Rd.
Creve Coeur 63141
(314) 576-6606
Open: Monday through Saturday,
7:30 AM–9:00 PM (Monday until 6:00 PM)

La Bonne Bouchée produces exquisite classic French breads, rolls, pastries, and chocolates. The French bread is crusty outside and light and flavorful inside. Croissants are perfect—flaky, buttery, and elastic. The almond croissant is stuffed with smooth almond paste and is decorated with sliced almonds and icing. Mini-brioches are rich with eggs and butter. Shell shaped madeleines, the tiny cakes that Marcel Proust loved, are tender, buttery, and flavorful morsels. The fruit tartlettes are beautiful as well as delicious. Seasonal fruit such as rhubarb, strawberries, and raspberries or various combinations of fruit are perched upon a mound of rich, light custard and whipped cream flavored with a touch of kirsch which is nestled in a buttery rich and crisp tart shell and finished with an apricot glaze. To accommodate American tastes, the tartlettes are larger and have more generous amounts of fruit than the traditional French ones. La Bonne Bouchée uses locally grown fruits when they are available. The chocolate mousse pastry begins with a layer of dark chocolate cake that is topped with rich chocolate mousse that literally bursts up out of its foil cup and is crowned with piped whipped cream. It is delicious and elegant. The truffles at La Bonne Bouchée are sublime—creamy and intensely chocolatey, they are dipped in a dark chocolate coating. The bakery has a beautiful selection of cakes and pies. Most dramatic is the chocolate mousse cake decorated in dark chocolate ribbons and ruffles. Other cakes that are good selections include those with lemon filling or fresh strawberries and cream.

Lake Forest Pastry Shop
7737 Clayton Rd.
Clayton 63117
(314) 863-7400
Open: Monday through Saturday, 7:00 AM–6:00 PM

There's always a line at this popular neighborhood bakery. The bakery has a large selection of pastries, some of which are good. Unfortunately, some are not. Try the pecan crunch ring, a very good coffee cake made with sweet Danish dough, four kinds of nuts, and a rich caramel icing. A large refrigerated case holds a selection of tortes, the real whipped cream cakes that are so popular at this bakery. This is a good place to buy a child's birthday cake, as the bakery does nice decorations and the cake is tasty. Some of the cookies are quite good. The bakery makes holiday concoctions for kids with lots of frosting and chocolate icing, cakes that look good to kids, but are tasteless. On Fridays, you can buy a loaf of good challah.

Mayer's Bakery and Catering Service
2903 S. Jefferson
St. Louis 63118
(314) 772-1600
Open: Friday and Saturday, 8:00 AM–5:00 PM

St. Louis has two distinct generations of quality bakers. The first are the bakers who brought their craft from the old country, and in an unbroken chain, practice their craft. The second younger type of baker is perhaps a backlash from the "Wonder Bread" years. These bakers are going back to the basics of good bread and pastry making and adding their generation's own nuances to their craft. At Mayer's Bakery there is no mistaking which generation is baking: John Mayer has elevated his craft to a fine art at this finest of St. Louis's old European-style bakeries. Here you will find a variety of perfect bread, each distinctive and born of the tradition of Mayer's native Germany. The rye bread has the full-bodied flavor of the grain transported to the taste buds in a moist loaf with a crisp thin crust. The beautiful, bountiful loaf called kranzkuchen is totally unique—an egg bread infused with the flavor of fresh nutmeg and sweetened with golden raisins. If there is any left over, it makes wonderful breakfast toast or French toast. Even the white bread at Mayer's is a treat; it has a delicious crisp crust and a moist smooth center. Cream bread, a white bread with cream, is fine textured, moist, and rich. And lenten bread, a huge flat loaf, has a chewy crust with a smooth, soft texture and lots of flavor.

The pastry at Mayer's is as exquisite as it is delicious. Strudels and stollens predominate. If your favorite stollen is poppy seed, here you can find an excellent, moist one. If you crave the sweet tartness of cherry strudel, the cherries are bliss and the pastry is flaky. How about cheese strudel? Mayer's cheese filling is rich and creamy, with just the right touch of vanilla and cinnamon. The cherry pecan stollen is a beautiful pinwheel design with fresh pecans and tart cherries. Prune horns are flaky with lots of sweet pureed prunes. Even a simple sweet pretzel has the tenderest of pastry and a drizzle of icing. You can find caramel rolls, donuts, sweet rolls, dinner rolls, and much more—and all for a pittance. Ten dollars will buy you a bag loaded with fresh bread and pastries. Mayers bakes with eggs that are fresh from a local farm and sells these eggs by the dozen. For the holidays there is a large selection of tasty Christmas cookies and, of course, Christmas stollen. A sign that appears on the wall during holidays "Let us bake your poultry or ham" announces a service provided at Mayer's that was brought from the old country and that reminds us of the nocturnal life of the neighborhood bakery. Mayer's Bakery and Catering Service is open only on Friday and Saturdays, which could be a sad omen for St. Louis. Run, don't walk, to sample the classic art of European baking before it's too late.

Miss Hullings
1103 Locust
St. Louis 63101
(314) 436-0840
Open: Monday through Saturday, 7:00 AM–5:00 PM
Other locations at: Plaza Frontenac (314) 997-3711,
St. Louis Centre (314) 621-4340 (call for hours)

The St. Louis tradition of celebrating a birthday with a "split cake" from Miss Hullings is a grand one. Depending on your mood, try either the chocolate or lemon. Moist and tender yellow cake is split into six layers with either dark rich chocolate or sweet-tart lemon frosting. The cakes come in either round or loaf shapes. If you want a round cake, be sure to call and order one. Loaf shaped cakes are usually on hand at the bakeries.

Missouri Baking Company
2027 Edwards St.
St. Louis 63110
773-6566
Open: Tuesday through Saturday, 7:00 AM–5:30 PM,
Sunday, 7:30 AM–noon

This old family bakery on the Hill has a large selection of pastries, cookies, and breads, but it is the outstanding selection of cookies and biscotti that make this bakery worthy of a special trip. Try the cuccidadi, predecessors of fig newtons, which are a local Italian specialty. These large wonderful cookies have a vanilla flavored dough wrapped around a gooey filling of figs, citrus, raisins, nuts, bits of chocolate and whatever else might be on hand when they are made. The display case boasts a large selection of tea cookies that are as delicious as they are beautiful. Included in this assortment are biscotti. The apricot-almond biscotti are delicious, with crunchy almonds and tart gooey apricots adding contrasting textures and flavors to the hard cookie. The chocolate biscotti are also wonderful. They are a not-too-sweet dark chocolate with chewy cherries. The regular biscotti with just a touch of anise, have nuts and fruit and are also very good. The biscotti are usually still soft when you buy them, but will dry out in a day or two—if you can keep them that long. Amaratti, almond-flavored meringue cookies, have a crisp almond flavor, but also need time to dry out in order to enjoy the smooth crunchy texture of the meringue. Tiny chocolate macaroons are chewy but low on chocolate flavor. Pecan-butter cookies are melt-in-your mouth rich, and unusual sesame cookies add a less sweet but nutty flavor to the assortment. During the holidays, specialty cookies are available.

The coffee cakes, which are made with a moist sweet dough and covered with a variety of toppings, including cheese and assorted fruits, are also good. The cheese Danish has a sweet and creamy filling and a thick icing. Some other good pastries are the custard creme puff, which has a light custard in a crunchy pastry puff sprinkled with sugar, and a Grand Marnier Napolean which has a good flaky pastry and a strong orange-flavored custard. The cannoli has a crunchy shell but its filling is not cheesy enough and it is low on bits of fruit or chocolate.

Pan Dora
1858 Russell
St. Louis 63104
(314) 773-6161
Open: Monday through Saturday, 7:00 AM–6:00 PM

Pan Dora is one of the outstanding bakeries in St. Louis. Its owners are part of a new generation of bakers who are going back to traditional (and time-consuming) baking techniques and adding a passion for quality and a reverence for process in order to produce outstanding baked goods. Pan Dora has breads, rolls, muffins, tea breads, cookies, and various brownies.

The ingredients used in the products are all natural and as fresh as can be. The whole grain flour used is milled on the premises, and the breads are shaped by hand. Quality ingredients and time make the labor-intensive products at Pan Dora so outstanding. There are special breads that they make only on certain days of the week. Just when you've finally chosen your favorite Pan Dora bread, you'll go to pick it up on a day of the week that you haven't been before only to discover Anna bread or olive bread and then you'll have a new favorite. Bakers bread is the name of Pan Dora's white loaf. It also comes in a whole wheat variety. Either long or round, the crusty loaf is flavorful and chewy. Biga is a sourdough white bread made with some whole wheat and rye: It is a hearty Italian style loaf. Blackstrap rye is a unique black bread mellowed with the flavors of molasses and orange zest. If you think of corn bread as dry and crumbly, think again. Pan Dora's version, Anna bread, is a moist, sweet (but not too sweet) loaf with a touch of molasses. It makes great peanut butter and jelly sandwiches and toast. Pan Dora's version of focaccia looks like small pizzas. They are tasty flattened breads made with olive oil. One of the basic types of focaccia is studded with fresh rosemary needles, brushed with olive oil, and sprinkled with salt. Other variations have such toppings as sage and garlic, black olive and red pepper, fresh eggplant and Asiago cheese, sun-dried tomato and mozzarella cheese, and Gorgonzola cheese.

Pan Dora has muffins, tea breads, and an especially delicious orange yeast roll that has a gooey center made with fresh orange rind. Other delicious citrus flavored pastries are the lemon bar, made with a buttery shortbread crust and a tart gooey lemon filling, and the lemon butter cookie, two very delicate and tender butter cookies sandwiching a powerful sweet-tart lemon filling. Other cookie and brownie selections that are very good include shortbreads, biscotti, chocolate murder cookies, and deep-chocolate walnut brownies.

Pastries of Denmark
12633 Olive Blvd.
Creve Coeur 63141
(314) 469-7879
Open: Monday through Friday, 7:30 AM–7:00 PM
and Saturday 8:00 AM–6:00 PM
Another location at: Northwest Plaza
(314) 344-0494 (call for hours)

Exquisite European pastries with distinct northern European influence give this bakery and café its unique character. Danish coffee cakes called *kringles* and *spandauers*, Danish butter cookies, and elegant fancy pastries are among the specialties of this wonderful bakery. *Kringles* are large coffee cakes with flaky pastry, fruit, nut, or cheese fillings, and vanilla or chocolate icings. The cherry chocolate kringle is delicious with its tart cherries and chocolate icing. A cheese Danish features a delicious custardy cheese filling in a tender sweet dough. The butter cookies are crisp vanilla cookies in pressed shapes that come with a variety of fillings or dips such as chocolate and pistachio, apricot, and raspberry. Chocolate, almond, and coconut play an important role in the bakery's fancy pastries. Many of them come miniaturized as petit fours, giving you an opportunity to sample a variety. Whether you buy it in an individual serving or as a petit four, don't miss the Sarah Bernhardt, a beautiful moist almond macaroon, topped with a rich chocolate truffle and enrobed in a shell of dark chocolate. The white chocolate version of the Sarah Bernhardt is equally delicious. A lemon slice petit four with its crispy lemon cake layered with lemon buttercream and topped with dark chocolate and a miniature lemon slice is an unusual treat. Other possibilities include French waffles, meringue balls, rum balls, marzipan chocolate logs, and double-chocolate truffle tortes. Pastries of Denmark has breads, some of which are good. The walnut wheat bread has a nice flavor. Others have good crusts but unfortunate cottony textures.

Pratzel's Bakery
928 N. McKnight
University City, 63132
(314) 991-0708
Open: Sunday through Friday, 7:30 AM–5:30 PM,
Friday until 4:30 PM and Sunday until 3:00 PM
Another location at: 727 N. New Ballas, Creve Coeur
(314) 567-9197 (call for hours)

This Kosher bakery has the best challah in town. The rye bread is a little short on rye flavor, but the moist dense texture, crispy thin crust, and crunchy tzitzle (cornmeal) sprinkled on the bottom make it an overall good bread. Tzitzle bread comes in large round loaves and is the same rye bread with caraway seeds and a sprinkling of tzitzle over the crust. Pratzel's has traditional holiday pastries, some of which are good, and some of which are not. The honey cake for the Jewish New Year is fine, but the Purim hamantaschen are wanting: only the poppyseed filled one is good, the prune filled pastry has a peculiar flavor of bottled lemon juice. The mandel bread is tasty and the kichel is dry—but isn't all kichel? For a tasty treat try the cherry flips: crispy, sugary elephant ears flipped over and filled with a bit of sour cherry filling.

Wei Hong Bakery and BBQ
8148 Olive Blvd.
University City 63130
(314) 993-6208
Open: Daily, 9:00 AM–8:00 PM

Wei Hong has a large selection of authentic Chinese pastries, some sweet and some savory. It also has fresh barbecue duck and pork. Here you will find traditional sweet pastries such as mooncakes, cookie-shaped pastries with lovely molded designs and filled with bean paste or lotus paste; crystal cakes made from sticky rice flour and bean paste; winter melon cakes; sesame bean balls; spicy cookies made with sesame seeds and sticky rice; lotus buns; custard buns; almond buns; and almond cookies. Savory pastries include buns filled with BBQ pork, curry beef, and chicken. There are deep fried pork dumplings, and taro root puffs made with rice flour. There are buns ready for you to steam, filled with BBQ pork, bean paste and louts paste. Some dim sun specialties are also made here such as dumplings stuffed with shrimp or pork, rice noodles, and lotus leaf with sticky rice, sausage, and green beans. The pastries at this bakery are totally unique and are wonderful with afternoon tea or as a finish to your own authentic Chinese meal.

Restaurants

Annie Gunn's
16806 Chesterfield Airport Rd.
Chesterfield 63017
(314) 532-3314
Open: Tuesday through Sunday,
11:00 AM–10:00 PM
(Friday and Saturday until 11:00 PM
and Sunday noon–7:00 PM)
Price range: Inexpensive to moderate

The whole country watched the national news with horror as Thom and Jane Sehnert were rescued from the roof of their restaurant after unsuccessfully attempting to save their business from the ravages of the great flood of 1993. The task of rebuilding is over and Annie Gunn's (and the Smoke House Market next door) is joyfully back. The restaurant is serving the same great food as always.

For an appetizer try the delicately smoked trout, which is smoked at the Smoke House Market. It is served with a slightly hot, creamy horseradish sauce, a few capers, and sweet red onions. Another good choice is chicken wings—breaded and crisply fried before being smothered in a Louisiana-style hot sauce and served with a creamy blue cheese dressing for dipping. The dinner salad of mixed greens is simple and fresh. The meat at Annie Gunn's is outstanding. Try the lamb chops, two thick chops that have been marinated in a slightly sweet marinade and seared on the outside: they are juicy and delicious. A peppered filet, with cracked peppercorns coating the outside, gives this tasty, tender steak an interesting bite. Other meat possibilities include smoked pork chops, barbecue baby back ribs, and Smoke House Market hamsteaks. Entrees come with a house salad, a baked potato or wild and white rice mixture, and fresh seasonal vegetables. They also serve a variety of chicken entrees as well as sandwiches. Annie Gunn's, although in a bar, has a kid's menu. The hearty and delicious hamburger and thick fries will make any hamburger-loving kid happy. The restaurant has a small but adequate wine list.

Arcelia's Mexicana Restaurant
2501 S. 9th at Victor
St. Louis 63104
(314) 776-5900
Open: Sunday through Thursday, 7:00 AM–9:00 PM,
Friday and Saturday until 10:30 PM
Price range: Inexpensive

Arcelia's has some very good authentic Mexican dishes, as well as some Americanized versions of Mexican food. The salsas at Arcelia's are good and authentic. The red salsa is smooth and made with flavorful dried chilis. The green salsa is made with fresh peppers, lime, and tomatillos. Both use chilis to flavor the salsa, rather than just to burn your tongue, and both are hot, with the green salsa the hotter of the two. Arcelia's makes good guacamole; it is creamy and chunky at the same time and has a touch of garlic, onion, and fresh tomato. Try the guacamole with green salsa—the guacamole cools your palate and allows you to taste the flavors of the salsa. Skip the botanas, a boring assortment of small appetizers made with flour tortillas and cheese or beans.

For a tasty Mexican dish that is not on many American menus, try the *albondigas*, cumin and chili spiced meatballs served with rice and refried beans or in soup. Another unusual dish is *nopales*, cactus stir fried with tomato and onions. The cactus tastes a bit like green pepper with a slightly sour note. You can order it with scrambled eggs or homemade *chorizo* (sausage). Arcelia's makes very good *chiles poblanos* (oftentimes called *chiles rellenos*); large green peppers stuffed with cheese or meat, dipped in egg batter, deep fried, and served under a rich brown gravy. Empanadas have a good meat filling but are in a strange heavy fried bread dough. All entrees are served with good rice, beans, and tortillas. Arcelia's has Mexican beer, which is served with a wedge of lime. The restaurant has a patio for dining in nice weather.

Bar Italia
4656 Maryland
St. Louis 63108
(314) 361-7010
Open: Tuesday through Sunday, 11:30 AM–midnight
(Sunday until 9:30 PM), dessert and coffee only after 9:30 PM
Price range: Moderate

Bar Italia is one of the best restaurants in St. Louis. It is the kind of place you can go to often—for a salad or plate of pasta for lunch, for a three or four course meal for dinner, or for coffee and dessert after a movie. You can go there alone and read the paper. You can take children, who are treated as people, or you can go for a great meal after a hard week at work. Everyone is made to feel welcome. This casual bustling restaurant is a hybrid of three types of establishments you find in Italy—a coffee bar, a trattoria, and a gelateria. And amazingly, it succeeds as all three.

Bar Italia has some terrific appetizers. Carpaccio combines the subtle flavor of very fresh slices of paper-thin raw beef with earthy olive oil and tangy capers, the bite of cracked pepper, and the sweet nuttiness of Parmigiano. Another good choice is *olive e formaggi*, a selection of imported cheeses such as sweet Gorgonzola, salty ricotta salata, and nutty Parmigiano are served with three types of olives, peppers, and crusty bread. A bit of olive oil is nice with this appetizer if the cheeses in the selection are not creamy. Other tempting items on the appetizer list are a stew with calamari, chick peas, and potatoes; goat cheese with crushed pepper and dried olives; and caponata, made with eggplant, olives, capers, and raisins. The homemade soup of the day is another tempting choice. Some of the possibilities include a delicate bean soup with greens, white beans, crisp celery and other vegetables; a tomato-based chicken barley soup that has a good flavor and consistency. Salads at Bar Italia have fresh greens that are cleaned and dried perfectly before they are coated with vinaigrette. A sprightly lemony vinaigrette makes the simple house salad (which comes with entrees) special. A few olives, a bit of cracked pepper, and perhaps a tomato wedge or radicchio add interest to the salad. When tomatoes are in season a wonderful salad choice is *caprese*, a tomato salad with fresh mozzarella, basil vinaigrette, and olives.

Pasta dishes compete with lamb, veal, chicken, and seafood offerings in the list of main courses. *Tortellini alla panna* is a simple classic dish made with both green and white tortellini filled with meat. The pasta is in a nutmeg scented cream sauce with bits of prosciutto, mushrooms, and peas. *Fettuccine tre amici* is a delicious dish; a hearty stew of Italian sausage, veal, and chicken in a tomato-based sauce, it is served over pasta. *Scaloppine alle erbe* is a wonderful choice, with slices of veal topped with pine nuts, raisins, and cheese, cooked with a savory blend of garlic, herbs, and wine, and served with a sauce of pureed red peppers. The lamb loin chops have a wonderful flavor from the wine marinade and mint-balsamic glaze, but can be a bit tough. Ask if the mussels are fresh. If so, the mussels steamed in a tomato-wine sauce are great. Don't be shy about dunking crusty bread in this delicious sauce—it's perfect for dunking.

The flavors of the Mediterranean are abundant in the desserts at Bar Italia. Figs, almonds, hazelnuts, lemons, and wine, combine with chocolate, cheese, rice, and cream to create these unique treats. As in Italy, the desserts are not overly sweet. Instead they rely on the natural flavors of the ingredients. The gelato is creamy, smooth, and full of natural flavor. Especially delicious are hazelnut gelato, with a smooth texture and intense flavor of hazelnuts, and the chocolate gelato, made with outstanding European chocolate that is not masked by too much sugar. The sorbets are made with the unmistakable flavors of fresh fruit. Both sorbets and gelatos are served in a tall stemmed glass with a cookie. A fig torte is absolutely unique and delicious with its naturally sweet figs and slightly astringent pine nut filling in a lattice-crusted pastry. The classic combination of chocolate and hazelnuts is found in an excellent torta gianduia, a rich and somewhat heavy flourless torte. For a lighter textured and sweeter torte, try torta vesuvio, made with sponge cake soaked in amaretto, vanilla cream, nuts, and chocolate. *Torta di riso* has rice custard layered between chocolate and almonds with a touch of orange zest and is very different. Other interesting possibilities are *torta de limone,* a lemon custard pie with a wedge of chocolate and pistachio, and *torta de pere,* a custard pie topped with pears poached in Marsala wine.

Bar Italia has a decent selection of "good value" Italian wines, as well as espresso drinks and cold beverages.

Bar Jamaica Jerk Pit-Cater Jamaica

8631 Olive St. Rd.
University City 63132
(314) 576-6160
Open: Daily, 11:30 AM –8:30 PM
(Sunday noon until 6:30 PM)
Price range: Inexpensive

The small storefront restaurant moved to a new location and is doing mostly take out of its delicious Jamaican home style cooking. Jerk-style Jamaican barbecue is made by marinating meat or fish in a sauce of Jamaican peppers, herbs, and spices, roasting it, and then smoking or barbecuing it to finish. The jerked chicken is delicious, moist, and spicy. The curried goat and curried chicken are good choices with their fork-tender meat stewed in a medley of spices and served on a bed of rice and peas with a tangy simple salad. An outstanding dish is the steamed red snapper with okra: the tender fish filet is served with crisply stewed okra, peppers, tomatoes, and onions on a bed of rice. The sampler platter allows you to try four or five main courses and an appetizer. The saltfish fritter appetizer and the Jamaican beef patty are a bit disappointing, but the meals are wonderful. So, although you can't sit and relax to the tropical beat while sipping a Jamaican beer at this new location, you can take it home and create your own little tropical paradise.

Café Provencal
40 N. Central
Clayton 63105
(314) 725-2755
Open: Monday through Saturday,
11:00 AM–2:00 PM (Saturday closed for lunch)
and Wednesday through Saturday 6:00 PM–10:00 PM
Price range: Moderate

The small storefront restaurant, with its brick walls and white tablecloths, is spare of decoration. The restaurant's no-nonsense approach to its decor and even to its menu which has such items as "tossed green stuff" and "that chocolate caramel walnut thing" lets you know that the chef chooses to spend his time preparing food rather than decorating or writing menus. It is probably this focus on food, coupled with a very small but well-thought-out menu that allows this restaurant, which has fewer than fifty seats and very reasonable prices, to survive in high-rent Clayton. It is noisy and crowded, so it is not a place to go for a quiet intimate meal. The menu changes seasonally, ensuring you of the freshest food available.

The bold and earthy flavors of the south of France are evident in the restaurant's generous use of herbs, onions and leeks, and fresh tomatoes. One of the selections you might find on the menu includes a wonderful onion tart that has a light flaky crust and is full of crisp sweet onions and an occasional anchovy. It is served with tossed greens in a sprightly vinaigrette. There may be the pissenlet salad, which contains curly endive and boiled red potato chunks, pieces of crisp bacon, thinly sliced onions, and a warm vinaigrette. The curly endive is able to withstand the warm vinaigrette without wilting and adds texture to this delicious salad. Sometimes, potato-leek soup is available, creamy and mild with chunks of potato.

Herb-roasted chicken makes a dramatic entrance with a mountain of perfectly cooked *pommes frites* ("French" fries), sliced like matchsticks and crisp throughout, that poke out in all directions, inviting you to take one. The half chicken is tender and moist and covered in a wonderful herb mixture, predominated by tarragon. Lightly flavored with lemon and leek, a filet of sea bass is served on a bed of couscous, with a delicious herb-crusted baked fresh tomato and buttered carrots. Roasted and tender slices of veal are served with fluffy and peppery mashed potatoes with their flavorful skins blended in and a few slices of chanterelle mushroom in an indistinct sauce.

You can almost forgive the soggy bottom crust of the pear tart because of the delicious and subtle combination of almond and pear, but, alas, humid weather might just be the death knell of this delicate classic French pastry. Much better able to withstand humidity is the nothing-delicate-about-it "chocolate caramel walnut thing." Rich with buttery, gooey caramel and fresh walnut chunks, this outstanding dessert has a crunchy shortbread type crust and a shell of dark bittersweet chocolate.

Café Provencal's prix fixe menu makes it an outstanding value. The wine list is very well suited to the menu. Reservations for dinner are a must.

Café Zoë
12 N. Meramec
Clayton 63105
(314) 725-5554
Open: Monday through Saturday, 11:30 AM–2:00 PM
and 5:00 PM–9:00 PM (Saturday closed for lunch and
Friday and Saturday open later)
Price range: Moderate to expensive

A light hand and a sophisticated menu make Café Zoë a grand adventure. As with all good adventures, taking risks enhances the experience. At Café Zoë, you can expand your culinary experience by taking a chance, or if you prefer, play it a bit safer. Café Zoë has a distinct style—with fresh herbs playing a vital role. Fresh chopped Italian parsley is used like confetti on the large plates, inviting you to celebrate your food. Chives are crisscrossed with a haphazard look that is not haphazard at all.

Other fresh herb garnishes poke out from arrangements of vegetables that are used for color as well as for flavor.

A simple, yet elegant appetizer is baked chèvre, in which the sweet mellow flavor of roasted garlic pairs well with the pungent flavor of goat cheese, the intense earthy flavor of sun-dried tomatoes, and the salty tang of capers. Olive oil and large toast triangles presented in a dramatic spoke-wheel pattern pull the flavors together in this excellent selection. Another wonderful choice is charred yellowfin tuna that is cooked rare and served with ginger vinaigrette. Duck cakes, made with duck meat and tangy dried cherries and served with homemade mayonnaise on a bitter green, are an unusual and tasty appetizer. An appetizer of salmon potato pancakes has a very good white butter sauce but could use a bit more salmon.

Café Zoë has a diverse selection of entrees. There is a risotto of the day. One of the very good risottos is made with fresh scallops, sun-dried tomatoes, fresh herbs, and fresh spinach. Grilled sea scallops is a unique Caribbean-inspired creation. Six large, perfectly grilled sea scallops are nestled between crisp unembellished black beans and savory papaya chutney and served with beautiful grilled vegetables and a thick delicious potato pancake. A very good chicken breast, stuffed with goat's-milk cheese and served with a piquant oregano vinaigrette, is cooked perfectly on the grill and served with a selection of grilled vegetables. For a rich and intensely flavored dish, try the grilled veal chop with onion marmalade. The reduced veal stock and sherry wine make a rich satisfying sauce that mixes well with the onion marmalade.

Sorbets make a nice dessert. The passion fruit sorbet has the exotic full flavor of passion fruit. The green apple sorbet is good with its sour apple note, but the lemon is not special. Sorbets are served with crisp biscotti. Café Zoë's version of tiramisu is a good one. The ingredients, sponge cake with liqueur, mascarpone cheese, and a dusting of chocolate are nicely proportioned and subtle.

The restaurant has a good selection of California wines that are offered at reasonable prices. You can purchase them by the bottle or glass.

California Pizza Kitchen
1439 Saint Louis Galleria
Richmond Heights 63117
(314) 863-4500
Open: Daily, 11:30 AM–10:00 PM, Friday and
Saturday until 11:00 PM, Sunday noon–9:00 PM
Price range: Inexpensive

Every region of the country has its own style of pizza that locals yearn for no matter where they settle. The California Pizza Kitchen's pizza is able to get beyond regional preference because the foundation of its pizza, the dough and the sauce, are excellent, and it adds some of the gutsiest combinations of fresh ingredients available. If you're not too tired from shopping, sit at the counter so you can watch the spectacle of the chefs creating these savory pies and sending them into the wood-fired oven. Like a great piece of bread, the dough is crisp, elastic, and flavorful. The list of topping combinations is plentiful and complicated. A few good choices are duck sausage, fresh spinach, sun-dried tomatoes, and roasted garlic, or grilled eggplant slices with red onions baked and then covered with a salad of uncooked fresh spinach, rehydrated sun-dried tomatoes and cilantro, and served with a vinaigrette. Some of the tantalizing ingredients you will find on the pizza menu are tandoori chicken, goat cheese, roasted sweet peppers of various colors, artichokes, shrimp, pesto, Peking duck, barbecue chicken, Jamaican banana chutney, and homemade black beans. If you don't want anything quite so exotic, you won't miss out by eating the savory traditional cheese pizza, another great choice. The restaurant also serves a host of fresh salads and desserts and has a children's menu.

Cardwell's
8100 Maryland
Clayton 63105
(314) 726-5055
Open: Monday through Saturday,
11:45 AM–3:00 PM and 5:45 PM–10:00 PM
(Friday and Saturday until 11:00 PM)
Price range: Expensive

A warm wood interior, tile floors, and white tablecloths give Cardwell's a rich clubby appearance, but this is one club to which everyone is welcome. In fact, far too much is made of the important people who frequent Cardwell's, and not enough is said about the important work going on in the kitchen. The menu is a wonderful blend of updated classics and unique creations from seasonal cuisine for the more adventurous. An example of updated classic appetizers is the duck pâté sampler. This selection includes a rich satiny-smooth mousse, a coarse country-style pâté with prune and cognac, and a slice of rillettes, served with peppery arugula and sweet pepper salad instead of traditional cornichons. Mellow, smoked Irish salmon is served with pickled vegetables, black bread, and horseradish cream. Fried spiced shrimp add a new twist to classic Ceasar salad.

A wonderfully prepared entree, grilled free-range chicken breast with fresh figs and spiced walnuts is served with a spicy salad of green and red lettuces, and a mountain of crisp straw potatoes. A more daring entree is scallops in Thai curry, which uses the contrasting flavors and textures of Thai cuisine with perfectly cooked meaty scallops. In-house-smoked pork tenderloin is updated with a sauce of Jack Daniels bourbon, mustard, and maple syrup and served with roasted onions and multi-grain pilaf. Filet mignon is available, as are other preparations of fish, seafood, duck, and lamb. Entrees are served with fresh seasonal vegetables. Cardwell's has a small selection of desserts. Try the very rich macadamia and white chocolate soufflé cake with its dense cake, whole macadamia nuts, and large shavings of white chocolate on a buttery caramel sauce. Cardwell's has a nice selection of wine that is appropriate for its menu.

China Royal
5911 N. Lindbergh (at McDonnell Blvd.)
Hazelwood 63042
(314) 731-0047
Open: Daily, 11:00 AM–9:30 PM
Price range: Inexpensive

In James Clavell's *Tai Pan*, a novel of Hong Kong, Clavell describes the first encounter between his protagonist and a powerful Chinese pirate, a meeting in which dim sum is served and the ritual of handling the delicate rice dough pastries with chopsticks sets the stage for "loss of face" and other power manipulations. You don't have to worry about losing face if you can't use chop sticks perfectly, because forks are available at China Royal, where you can participate in a superb meal which has centuries old ritual meaning. Dim sum are small delicacies, many of which are made with rice dough and stuffed with meat, seafood, and vegetables. They are steamed or deep fried. You are served from rolling carts which come along every few minutes with small steaming plates of delectables. Although sometimes the same items are wheeled by, if you stay long enough, you will be astonished by the variety. With more than 35 possibilities, it's good to go with a group, so you can taste many of the dishes.

Steamed buns filled with meat and vegetables, rice noodles filled with meat or shrimp, delicate rice dumplings also filled with meat or shrimp, and spring rolls made with crisp vegetables and meat are some of the tasty standards. But for those with a yearning for the unusual, try sticky rice in lotus leaves, a savory combination of sticky rice combined with succulent Chinese sausage, barbecue pork, shrimp, black mushrooms, or vegetables (not to mention whatever else the chef has around) wrapped in a large lotus leaf and steamed. Try eggplant stuffed with shrimp; or crisp, plump, deep-fried taro dumplings; or wonderful fried turnip cakes with Chinese sausage (how do they get lowly turnips to taste so good?); or green peppers stuffed with shrimp in black bean sauce; or deep-fried crab claws; or pork rolls with oyster sauce; or beef balls with watercress; or moist and tender BBQ quail and BBQ pork. If you have room, unusual desserts such as steamed lotus seed paste buns or sweet bean curd pudding, or coconut gelatin are unique sweet treats. Hot tea is good and plentiful, and although your table might be filled with stacks of empty dishes, your pocketbook will hardly notice.

Fio's La Fourchette
7515 Forsyth
Clayton 63105
(314) 863-6866
Open: Tuesday through Saturday,
6:00 PM–11:00 PM
Price range: Expensive

With many fine restaurants crowding the fine dining arena, Fio's is still the place to go for updated classic French cuisine served in a quiet tasteful ambience. You may choose a five-or-six-course fixed price meal or you may simply order off the menu. The menu features both cold and warm appetizers. Mussels, served chilled, in a piquant mustard sauce, are an excellent way to titillate your taste buds. An exquisitely presented appetizer of veal pâté and fennel aspic is an excellent choice. The pâté is smooth, rich, and slightly crunchy, thanks to the addition of crisp pistachio nuts. A mold of aspic with crisp fennel is served with a fresh creamy herb sauce spun into a flower design by very deft hands. Escargots perched atop giant shiitaki mushrooms in a creamy roasted garlic sauce are rich and satisfying. Crisp, meaty crawfish fritters are served with a creamy curry sauce that is nicely complemented by smoked oysters. Other interesting selections include venison carpaccio, paper-thin slices of raw venison served with Parmesan and herbs, and black pepper pasta with a coulis of root vegetables and artichoke.

Veal medallions make an outstanding entree, both in presentation and in intensity and clarity of flavor. Sautéed free-range veal is served with asparagus that is lightly breaded and fried crisp. A sauce made from veal stock, wine, and cream is rich and delicious. A lighter winning entree is the sautéed salmon. The brown butter gives this sauce an intense butter flavor, and capers add a welcome tang. The mild distinctive flavor of fresh grilled tuna is unfortunately masked by a too powerful mustard sauce. Entrees come with an nicely presented plate of vegetables prepared in a variety of ways. Other intriguing entrees include beef tenderloin with Gorgonzola cheese baked in puff pastry, sautéed foie gras in portobello mushroom powder with wild mushroom and black truffle oil ragoût. Salads are served after the main course and a simple salad of mixed autumn greens served with a light fresh vinaigrette and a sprinkling of toasted pecans is a good choice. After each course, your server offers you an additional portion of the course you've just consumed.

Fio's has some excellent desserts. Among the very special selections are the soufflés. The low-calorie molasses soufflé, served with eggnog custard, is light, flavorful, and very pretty. The ever popular white chocolate toffee torte is very sweet, with a graham cracker pecan crust, layer of white chocolate, and top layer of silky toffee. Excellent homemade hazelnut ice cream really satisfies with the concentrated flavor of hazelnuts, rich creamy texture, and chopped toasted nuts.

Fio's has a number of special menu features. Each day specific low fat menu selections are available (and identifiable on the menu). Each fall, during game season, the restaurant offers a game menu in addition to its regular menu. Such unusual items as antelope, elk, pheasant, caribou, moose, wild boar, venison, reindeer, rattlesnake, and black bear are available from the end of October until early December.

Fitz's Bottling Co.
6605 Delmar Blvd.
University City 63130
(314) 726-9555
Open: Daily, 11:30 AM–midnight
(Sunday noon–9:00 PM)
Price range: Inexpensive to moderate

Die-hard root beer lovers will love Fitz's and even root beer cynics might be won over to the brown brew produced and bottled at this unique micro-brewery and restaurant. The root beer is good—creamy and not too sweet. You may come to this family-friendly restaurant for the root beer, but you'll come back for the good food. The big surprise on this menu is the variety. Your kids can have good burgers and chili or a tasty barbecue brisket sandwich. The fries and crisp thick fried onion rings are good accompaniments. And you can have an unusual and very good grilled vegetable plate, which consists of fresh vegetables such as one night's array of three colors of sweet peppers, eggplant, asparagus, zucchini, summer squash, and one half of a huge portobello mushroom. You can get these same vegetables with Maryland crab cakes, two thick, spicy (if somewhat filler filled) crab cakes served with grilled vegetables and black bean salad. Other tempting menu items are southern fried catfish, smoked baby back ribs, and Dave's samurai salad.

The restaurant has kid's meals. Fitz's mixes its own soda flavors in cola, cherry cola, cream, ginger ale, lemon lime, orange, black cherry, cherry vanilla, and cherry ginger ale. They make interesting floats out of these sodas mixed with ice cream. Fitz's house float is root beer and French vanilla ice cream; a dreamsicle is orange soda and vanilla ice cream; an avalon is cream soda with coffee ice cream; and a dark and tan is cream soda with chocolate ice cream. Root beer is available in bottles to go.

King and I Restaurant
3157 South Grand
St. Louis 63118
(314) 771-1777
Open: Tuesday through Sunday,
11:30 AM–3:45 PM and 5:00 PM–9:45 PM
(Saturday and Sunday from noon)
Price range: Inexpensive

The King and I is an excellent place to enjoy the authentic flavors that make Thai cooking the cuisine of contrasts. Fiery peppers are cooled by the refreshing flavors of coconut milk and cucumbers; fresh crunchy vegetables are paired with soft tofu, and sour Thai spices clear your palate of the sweet flavors of fruit. Ingredients such as banana blossoms, galangal (a relative of ginger with a faint flavor of camphor), and lemongrass make these dishes complex and totally unique. The restaurant is large and pleasantly decorated. You can choose a regular table or sit in a sunken table on the floor with pillow back rests.

Satay makes a good appetizer. You can choose either pork or chicken, which will come to the table skewered and served with a peanut sauce and cucumber-red onion salad. The peanut sauce is mild and could use a bit more hot pepper. A large portion of crunchy tempura, in your choice of vegetable or sea food, is good. Hot and spicy dishes are indicated with asterisks, and you can order them mild, medium, or hot. If you order mild, you will not find a trace of the fiery peppers that are an important ingredient in Thai cuisine. Some of the entrees are stir fried and others are stew-like soups presented in bowls. *Tom yum ka-lum pe* is a wonderful complex dish of chicken in a soup of coconut milk, with chunks of banana blossom, slices of galangal, kaffir leaves, lemon grass, cilantro, lime, and spices. Other "tom yums" are made with fish, beef, or vegetables. *Kang daeng pak* is a very good vegetable entree with baby eggplant, snow peas, tofu, and other vegetables in a spicy red curry flavored coconut milk. For a very good stir-fried dish that combines the spices used in red curry with chicken, eggplant, sweet peppers, and fresh basil, try *pad ped kai.* Red curry duck has a good combination of flavors with its roast duck, pineapple, cherry tomatoes, green pepper, and basil in a hot-as-you-want-it red curry. The extensive menu includes such noodle dishes as *pad thai,* the tasty stir-fried rice noodle dish with bits of pork, shrimp, tofu, green onion, bean sprouts, and crunchy peanuts. Intriguing seafood possibilities include *pla koong,* a shrimp dish with lemon grass, red and green onion served in a spicy sour sauce and a seafood casserole of shrimp, mussels, crab, and squid cooked with spinach and bean threads in oyster sauce.

LoRusso's Cucina
3121 Watson Road
St. Louis 63139
(314) 647-6222
Open: Monday through Saturday, 11:00 AM–2:00 PM
and 5:00 PM–10:00 PM (Saturday closed for lunch)
Price range: Moderate

A great choice to eat on the Hill is really a few blocks off the Hill. LoRusso's menu has all of the classic Italian dishes you'd expect to find, plus a bevy of dishes that creatively combine Italian cuisine with current trends in lighter fare that are sure to become classics themselves. Some of the ingredients that appear on the menu in innovative combination include sun-dried tomatoes, eggplant, roasted garlic, fresh mozzarella, grilled fresh tuna, pesto, porcini mushrooms, fresh herbs, and artichokes.

Avoid the minestrone, which is not minestrone at all, but rather a salty beef stock with some watery vegetables. The house salad is tasty—head and romaine lettuces with a touch of red onion, shredded cheese, and pimento. The house vinaigrette is piquant and tasty.

LoRusso's red sauce, which is the foundation for many of its classic dishes, is very good. Unlike so many of the sauces found in other Italian restaurants, LoRusso's is not sickly sweet. The hearty sauce allows you to taste the flavor of tomatoes, and in fact, chunks of tomato are abundant in the pasta dishes. A very good traditional dish is lasagna, which has a good balance of pasta, tomato and meat sauce, and cheeses.

An excellent entree is the *vitello carciofi* (veal with artichokes). The dish consists of two large thin slices of veal, lightly dusted with flour that enables the dry white wine sauce to glaze the meat, which is enhanced by the earthy flavor of sliced artichoke hearts and intense flavor of chopped dried tomatoes. This is a dish to savor. The side dish of twice-baked potato with roasted garlic is a great choice. Potatoes are mashed with sweet roasted garlic and piped back into the potato skin before being baked again. Veal Parmesan and eggplant Parmesan more traditional dishes, are good choices. The veal is lightly breaded so you can taste the veal, and is topped with sauce and melted cheese in good proportion. The eggplant is not the least bit bitter and is lightly breaded and firm. Both are served with a side order of pasta; the red is a simple but good sauce with chunks of tomatoes, and the white is nicely garlicy with cheese and fresh parsley. The veal Parmesan sandwich on the lunch menu is a big disappointment. Unlike the real veal served on dinner entrees, this "veal cutlet" is an overly salted and breaded patty that should be avoided.

LoRusso's has a small selection of inexpensive and moderately priced wines, mainly from California. Dessert at LoRusso's is okay, but not great. Tiramissou is good, with a mild creamy but not very cheesy layer over a rum-soaked sponge cake that is too heavily dusted with cocoa. The crème brulée can have a grainy texture. A chocolate raspberry ice cream truffle combines the intense flavors of raspberry and chocolate in a rich dessert; raspberry sorbet is enrobed in chocolate ice cream and a shell of dark chocolate. For another dessert possibility, take a short drive to Ted Drewes Frozen Custard and indulge in a concrete (see Chocolates and Ice Cream section in this book.)

Mai Lee Restaurant
8440 Delmar
University City 63124
(314) 993-3754
Open: Tuesday through Sunday, 11:00 AM–9:00 PM
(Friday and Saturday until 10:00 PM)
Price range: Inexpensive

Soups and seafood are the big winners at this popular storefront Vietnamese restaurant. Large bowls of soup with various combinations of noodles, meat or seafood, and spices come to the table piping hot with smaller serving bowls and a plate heaped with beautiful fresh leafy lettuce leaves, sweet basil, bean sprouts, and lemon. An especially interesting soup, *bun nuoc leo*, is served on weekends only: it has noodles, seafood, and lemongrass in a spicy broth. *Goi cuon*, the cold egg rolls of shrimp, pork, and crisp vegetables, are tightly wrapped in rice paper and served with a spicy red sauce with chopped peanuts. The kitchen sends the entrees to the table artfully arranged. *Tom ram man* consists of fresh tail-on shrimp, stir-fried in a not-very-hot but very tasty red chili sauce, arranged with cool cucumber slices. Beware of the dried red chilis that sometimes hide in the fresh corkscrew pieces of squid, and that help flavor *muc xao cay*, a delicious squid and vegetable dish with a complex sauce. There are delicacies on the very extensive menu such as eel in lemongrass, steamed blue crab, frog with hot chili sauce, and chicken salad Vietnamese style. They serve a nice selection of Vietnamese coffee drinks and cold drinks made with blended tropical fruits, served in milkshake-sized glasses.

Nobu's Japanese Restaurant
8643 Olive St. Rd.
University City 63132
(314) 997-2303
Open: Daily except Wednesday,
weekdays 11:30–2:00 PM and 5:00 PM–9:30 PM,
weekends 5:00 PM–10:00 PM
Price range: Moderate

Nobu's serves delicious sushi and sashimi, those beautiful appetizer morsels of Japanese artistry. It also cooks up Japanese standards such as sukiyaki, tempura, and teriyaki. Sushi is the Japanese specialty that is based on boiled rice sweetened with rice vinegar and used in various combinations with raw fish, vegetables, pickles, tofu, and other ingredients. Sashimi, or sliced raw fish that is served with various condiments, is what people in the U.S. often mean when referring to sushi. Maki is sushi with rice, vegetables, fish, and any variety of ingredients wrapped tightly in thin sheets of seaweed. At Nobu's, you can inspect a picture menu and decide just how adventurous you want to be. Among your selections, be sure to try Nobu's California maki. It is served with transparently thin slices of pickled ginger and wasabi, the pale green Japanese fiery horseradish that you mix with soy sauce.

Nobu's does better with fresh raw fish than it does with cooked fish. A nice sauce cannot hide the disaster of an overcooked swordfish, and yosenabe, a Japanese-style bouillabaisse, is served so scalding that the delicate seafood continues to cook and becomes tough. Tempura is very good, but needs more and a larger variety of vegetables. A pan-fried noodle dish, yaki udon, is tasty and rich with sesame oil.

Original Wings N Things
1720 N. Kingshighway
St. Louis 63113
(314) 361-0661
Open: Daily, 10:00 AM–9:00 PM
(Friday and Saturday until midnight)
Price range: Inexpensive

The hot and spicy chicken wings are great—moist and tender inside, crisp and spicy outside. The lightly battered and fried wings have a spicy hot sauce that is absorbed into the wings, turning them red and keeping them crisp. They are served with additional Louisiana-style sauce, which has a piquant blend of spices and vinegar, and for those who like to live dangerously, there are "super hot" wings on demand. The "things" in the restaurant's name include three types of deep-fried fish—cat, buffalo, and jack (or whiting) which have crisp, crunchy cornmeal batter that stays crisp even after the fish cools off. The fish is fresh and perfectly cooked. Tasty fries are served with a little seasoned salt. Creamy sweet potato pie makes a nice ending to the meal. The restaurant also does a brisk take-out business for those looking for an alternative to take-out fast food.

Painted Plates
6235 Delmar
University City 63130
(314) 725-6565
Open: Wednesday through Sunday, 5:00 PM–11:00 PM
and until 1:00 AM Thursday through Saturday
Price range: Moderate

Painted Plates combines traditional American ingredients with an artful presentation, an American wine list that is matched to the menu, and a decor that is both relaxing and stimulating. Down-to-earth food rises to new heights at this well-thought-out restaurant that is elegant yet casual, and sophisticated yet earthy. Painted Plates is the perfect name for it, because each plate is a beautiful composition of food that delights the eye while pleasing the palate. Here, even an unwieldy lamb shank is arranged at just the right angle, with dollops of fresh spinach and a few deftly arranged whimsical fried pasta strands, to make a dramatic presentation. Served with hearty barley and wild mushrooms and topped with roasted garlic sauce, this entree that combines earthy flavors and succulent meat proves that presentation can be more than just a pretty face.

Large white plates provide the empty canvas for the food, much of which is quite humble fare, such as potatoes, barley, root vegetables, creamed peas, and long-cooked green beans that are transformed into edible works of art. A good appetizer of garlicy potato pancakes is dressed up with two cream-based sauces—one with chives lending a green color and the other with tomato giving it an orange hue— thinly striped in the perpendiculars of a plaid pattern. Another appetizer of seared rare tuna with cracked pepper crust sits atop a round of herbed toast; fresh spinach and thin stripes of red wine sauce provide both color and flavor contrasts. A simple salad of field greens in a light vinaigrette is pretty and satisfying. In addition to the lamb shanks, pecan-encrusted walleyed pike is an excellent entree. Tender fish is paired with rich pecans and butter sauce and served with delicious sweet potato purée and creamed peas and mushrooms. Poppy seeds add nuttiness to fresh pink salmon that is perfectly cooked and served with pretty green spinach, rosemary encrusted red potatoes, and just the right amount of not-overpowering Dijon mustard sauce. Du Da Betty's is an interesting pasta dish made with whole-wheat tube-shaped pasta and roasted vegetables combined with American goat cheese and toasted sunflower seeds.

For dessert, try apple cranberry crisp. This outstanding square of fruit covered in a crusty oatmeal pastry sits on top of a buttery caramel sauce with a plaid design of dark chocolate. Another excellent sweet is the warm blond brownie, topped with homemade espresso ice cream that is presented on top of a crème anglaise with a caramel and chocolate plaid design. Homemade vanilla ice cream makes a simple finish to a wonderful meal. Painted Plates is very reasonably priced and it is open late, allowing theater or concert goers an opportunity to eat late. This daring restaurant ups the ante on St. Louis restaurants, challenging others to rise to new heights.

Peking Inn
11923 Olive St. Rd.
Creve Coeur 63141
(314) 567-5534
Open: Daily, 11:00 AM–2:00 PM and
5:00 PM–9:30 PM
Price range: Inexpensive

The Peking Inn has a Korean menu (and Korean chef-owner). That is the reason to go to this restaurant. Good Korean food is a real treat, and you can find it here. For an appetizer, try *bin dae duk*. These tasty pancakes are made with mung bean flour and mixed vegetables, and have a unique earthy flavor. Ask for kimchi soup, which is on the menu, but not translated from the Korean. This fiery soup is made with kimchi, the fermented cabbage that is a Korean staple, tofu, and pork. Although spicy-hot, it is toned down for American tastes.

Bul go gi baek ban is a delicious entree of barbecued, marinated beef. It is tender, succulent, and rather sweet. *Nak ji bok um* is a flavorful dish of small octopus sautéed with onions and lots of white pepper. *Bi bim bap* comes to the table sizzling in its ceramic pot. This rice, vegetable, beef dish is served with a fried egg on top. Meals are served with a variety of interesting side dishes that are not shown on the menu and change daily. Fiery kimchi is sure to be one of them. Other possibilities include batter-dipped and fried zucchini with beef, pickled turnips, pickled seaweed and seafood, or pickled radish.

Royal Chinese BBQ
8406 Olive Rd.
University City 63130
(314) 991-1888
Open: Daily, 11:00 AM–9:30 PM,
(except Friday, Saturday, Sunday 10:30 AM–10:30 PM
and Sunday until 9:30 PM)
Price range: Inexpensive

Forget all of your old notions about Cantonese food, popularized in the seventies with such dull standbys as chop suey and chow mein made with overcooked bean sprouts and hard cardboard-like "fried " noodles. The Cantonese food served at the Royal Chinese BBQ might as well be from another planet —it's that different. This food is authentic Cantonese style barbecue, and it is served in modest surroundings.

It's not easy to figure out what's on the menu, because there are at least two menus, plus a blackboard full of specials. But if you're persistent and ask lots of questions, you will be rewarded with a terrific meal. Even such an old standard as eggrolls, commonly reduced to mushy cabbage filling a tough wonton skin, has an uncommonly good combination of chopped crispy vegetables and BBQ meat filling a tender and crunchy skin. Unusual pot stickers are made with slippery rice noodles stuffed with shrimp and crisp vegetables. A wonderful choice from the blackboard menu is "root leaf sea food pot." A huge lotus leaf lines a ceramic pot, where it embraces a stew of shrimp, scallops, crab sticks, fish balls, squid, black and straw mushrooms, bamboo shoot slices, green onions, snow peas, carrots, and Chinese cabbage. The stuffed lotus leaf is steamed in the pot and brought to the table for you to unfold while the scent of the filling escapes from the lotus leaf. The ingredients are fresh and succulent. Eggplant seafood pot is a similar but spicier dish.

The restaurant serves a variety of unique noodle dishes. Chow mein consists of your choice of sautéed meat or seafood and vegetables, such as bok choy and mushrooms, served atop a mountain of soft curly pan-fried noodles with a mild garlic flavored sauce. The chicken is tender white meat and the shrimp are fresh and plump. Although mild, this dish has lots of subtle texture and flavor. Another interesting rice dish is called "spicy thin rice noodles (Singapore style)." This flavorful dish is made with very thin noodles that are dry sautéed in a spicy curry mixture and mixed with plump shrimp, tender BBQ pork, green pepper, green onions, carrots, and black mushrooms. Of the noodle dishes, chow fun disappoints; the wide rice noodles are thick and bland, instead of silky and flavorful, and the green onions added with your choice of meat do not provide enough vegetable variety. Among the good menu items are General Tsao's chicken which is spicy hot with a very intensely flavored sauce. Large chunks of meat are breaded and served in a rich red sauce from which you should remove the red pepper slices unless you like very hot peppers. Other intriguing possibilities include steamed whole fish, chef's special roasted BBQ duck, shrimp dumplings and noodles (in soup), and various congees (soups) such as sliced abalone and chicken, or preserved egg and beef.

Sadie Thompson's Cafe
6347 N. Rosebury at DeMun
Clayton 63105
(314) 863-4414
Open: Tuesday through Saturday,
weekdays 11:00 AM–2:00 PM and 5:00 PM–9:00 PM,
and Friday and Saturday 5:00 PM–11:00 PM
Price range: Moderate

A light hand, fresh seasonal ingredients, and inventive preparation give this intimate storefront café its distinct style. Its neighborhood location just west of Forest Park, tucked among small antique stores, makes it a great lunch time escape or dinner hideaway. A delicious salad that you can have for lunch or light dinner combines fresh lettuces with marinated and grilled chicken breast slices, rich cashews, fresh fruit (orange or pear), and crisp snow peas. The gumbo, a spicy combination of tomato chunks, fresh fish, spicy Cajun sausage, shrimp, and crisp okra is especially good because the fish and vegetables are not over-cooked. The pâté sampler is a delicious showcase of the chef's range: the pâté maison is a rich light chicken liver mousse; the chicken pesto is a very fresh chicken salad lightly flavored with fresh basil and just the right amount of homemade mayonnaise; the Cajun seafood pâté combines chunks of fresh seafood, vegetable, and spices in a terrine for a delicate spreadable treat; salmon mousse pairs fresh salmon and sour cream with thinly sliced dill pickles. A variety of fresh breads is served with meals.

Happily for us, the chef at Sadie Thompson's evidently has an aversion to overcooking vegetables, meat, or fish, so fresh and tender are the order of the day. Coq au vin, the traditional French chicken and wine stew has a most inventive and delicious interpretation here: a very tender grilled chicken breast is topped with three fresh sautéed shrimp, pearl onions, and mushrooms in a light red wine sauce. A triangle of warm puff pastry tops the dish, which is served with wild and white rice and fresh vegetables. French country stew is another dish that eschews slow stewing methods for fresh last minute cooking and combining: tenderloin tips cooked medium rare and tender are combined with spicy sausage slices, tender chicken breast, red potatoes, and egg dumplings in a light sauce. All of the entrees are served with a variety of fresh, perfectly cooked vegetables. The menu has five entrees and each day there is a special or two, and although the menu is small, it succeeds at providing variety and freshness. Save room for dessert—the pastries are home-made by an expert. If *gerbot* is available, try this wonderful short dough pastry filled with apricot, chocolate, and ground pecans and walnuts. Pies have tender crusts and fresh fruits. There are hazelnut tortes, lemon cakes, and chocolate cakes. The restaurant has a small list of wines available by the glass, bottle, or split (small bottle, perfect for two).

Saleem's Lebanese Restaurant
6501 Delmar
University City 63130
(314) 721-7947
Open: Monday through Saturday, 5:00 PM–10:00 PM
(Friday and Saturday until 11:30 PM)
Price range: Inexpensive to moderate

Saleem's is a very exotic restaurant with lots of brass decorations, draped curtains, and Middle eastern music to set the tone. Its annual garlic festivals and "garlic king" motto really are superfluous because the restaurant has many types of genuinely good food year round. Most notably in the appetizers, you can enjoy the contrasting flavors and textures that make this cuisine special. The sour taste of lemon, the refreshing flavor of fresh parsley, the tang of olives, the earthiness of cracked wheat, the sweetness of garlic when it is roasted, and the bite of garlic when it is raw, are some of the flavors you can experience. The hummus, a ground chick pea and tahini dip is creamy and light, the baba ghanoush, another dip with eggplant and tahini, is spiced with garlic and fresh lemon. Saleem's version of tabbouleh salad has lots of chopped fresh parsley, a small amount of cracked wheat, and chopped tomato, onion, and lemon juice. It is a refreshing, flavorful salad. The falafel, deep fried fava bean patties spiced with cumin, are crunchy on the outside and smooth and light on the inside. They are served with a tasty tahini, yogurt, and lemon dressing and garnished with lots of parsley and radishes. The *mezza*, or assortment of appetizers, allows you to sample all of these appetizers, plus chunks of tangy feta cheese and good imported olives. The entrees consist mostly of marinated and broiled chicken, beef, or lamb served with rice. Sandwiches of falafel or marinated chicken or beef are served in pita bread with various tahini or garlic sauces. Desserts consist of your choice of baklava or halvah.

Sansui Japanese Restaurant
4955 West Pine Blvd.
St. Louis 63108
(314) 367-2020
Open: Monday through Friday, 11:30 AM–2:00 PM
and Monday through Saturday 5:30 PM–10:00 PM
(Friday and Saturday until 11:00 PM)
Price range: Moderate

A low lit sophisticated and quiet setting is the perfect place to eat the jewel-like morsels created at Sansui's sushi bar. The restaurant offers variety platters or individual servings of sushi and sashimi. Sashimi, or sliced raw fish that is served with various condiments, is what people in the U.S. often mean when they say "sushi." Sushi is actually the Japanese specialty that is based on boiled rice sweetened with rice vinegar and used in various combinations with raw fish, vegetables, pickles, tofu, and other ingredients. Maki is sushi with rice, vegetables, fish, and any variety of ingredients wrapped tightly in thin sheets of seaweed. It is served with transparently thin slices of pickled ginger and wasabi, the pale green Japanese fiery horseradish that you mix with soy sauce. Crisp grated daikon radish is often served with sashimi and adds texture to the dish. At Sansui, you can sample a variety of these delicacies that are made with fresh fish. For a delicious entree try the tempura. Fresh shrimp and a variety of vegetables that includes slices of sweet potato, onion, green bean, mushroom, and carrot, are fried in a light batter.

Sherman's Stage Deli
9641 Olive St. Rd.
Olivette 63132
(314) 991-5095
Open: Daily, Monday through Thursday, 6:00 AM–10:30 PM,
Friday and Saturday, 7:00 AM–1:00 AM, and
Sunday 7:00 AM–3:00 PM
Price range: Inexpensive

Sherman's is a nostalgic family-style Jewish restaurant with a bar and a piano player who, in the evening, sings snappy sing-along-if-you-like tunes. The restaurant serves breakfast, lunch, and dinner. The menu is extensive, with Jewish standards such as knishes, kishka, kasha, and kugel sharing the menu with tamales, toasted ravioli, and pizza. Most importantly, Sherman's serves good corned beef, pastrami, hard salami, and hot dogs. The corned beef and pastrami are served warm and moist, and the hard salami is cut thin enough that you won't break your teeth biting into it. Plump hot dogs in natural casing give them a juicy snap. Sandwiches come in three sizes, with the small size being enough for most people. The chicken soup is good and the matzo balls are tender and tasty, but the mushroom barley soup is pasty and bland. Omlettes are large, fluffy, and fresh. Baked chicken, brisket of beef, and cabbage rolls are a few of the dinner selections that come with enough food for two. The cabbage rolls are too sweet. Order your dinner with a side of tasty and moist kasha and shells. The cole slaw, creamy and crunchy, is good. Sherman's has other traditional Jewish favorites such as smoked fish, chopped liver, and borscht.

Sidney Street Café
2000 Sidney Street
St. Louis 63104
(314) 771-5777
Open: Tuesday through Saturday,
11:00 AM–3:00 PM (Saturday closed for lunch)
and 5:00 PM–9:45 PM (Saturday until 10:45 PM)
Price range: Moderate to expensive

The Sidney Street Café is an upscale restaurant housed in a beautifully renovated urban bar that serves very creative food. Brick walls, wood floors, tablecloths, and classical dinner music help create the sophisticated ambience. The menu reflects a diversity of origins, from European to Asian to Southwest American. Wake up you taste buds with the blue cheese tart appetizer. Silver-dollar-sized puff pastries successfully combine the intense flavors of blue cheese, walnuts, and pesto. Crab cake with tequila cream sauce is another good choice. Sweet corn adds to the delicate flavor of the crab, and the mild sauce has a touch of fresh cilantro. Sidney Street's dinner salad is simply the best; a fresh assortment of greens, artfully sliced vegetables, and homemade crunchy croutons provide a wonderful variety of flavor, texture, and color. Optional blue cheese crumbles and a good vinaigrette work to make this salad outstanding. Some of the other wonderfully enticing appetizers are café strudel filled with artichoke hearts, spinach and prosciutto; puff pastry escargot; and Thai shrimp.

The café's signature dish, poulet Montrachet, is worthy of its distinction. Tender and succulent, this chicken breast stuffed with fresh spinach leaves, prosciutto, artichoke hearts, and creamy goat's-milk cheese, is herb encrusted and served with a creamy wine-butter sauce. Another excellent entree is mixed seafood grill. One night's offering includes sea scallops, grilled crisp on the outside and moist and tender inside and served with a mellow roasted red pepper sauce, huge prawns stuffed with creamy goat's-milk cheese that cools off an accompanying peppery salsa with fresh parsley, and perfectly grilled tuna on a bed of pickled ginger. The entrees are presented beautifully with a variety of fresh vegetables playing an important role in the presentation. A savory blend of chewy wild and brown rice, with corn, sun-dried tomatoes, and herbs is covered with fresh spinach leaves for a distinctive addition to the bountiful plate. The café also has interesting veal, lamb, steak, and fish dishes. The wine list is small and the desserts are by Cravings, the wonderful pastry shop in Webster Groves. Most peculiar is the practice of servers reciting a litany of 20 or more menu items, which no customer can remember. When the room is noisy, the servers have to shout to be heard, making conversation by nearby diners impossible. Diners deserve a menu to peruse, and the fine menu deserves perusal.

The Tap Room
2100 Locust St.
St. Louis 63103
(314) 241-2337
Open: Daily, 11:00 AM–10:00 PM,
(Friday and Saturday until midnight and
Sunday noon–9:00 PM)
Price range: Inexpensive

You don't have to be a beer aficionado to love the beer brewed here and you don't have to be a gourmand to love the quality and creativity put into this unique pub-style menu. Ordinary foods such as chili, French fries, cole slaw, and even ketchup are made extraordinary. The restaurant is housed in an old red brick factory building. An appealing tile and oak bar adorns the large room, and a glass wall allows you to see the tops of the beer-making vessels of the downstairs microbrewery. They make about six beers, from pale pilsners, to amber ales, to heavy stouts, as well as seasonal brews. You can buy them by the pint or half-pint or try a sampler with a selection of five beers. To go with your beer, you have a choice of hearty pub food such as delicious, spicy white bean chili made with chicken, white beans, and flavorful peppers and served with a roasted jalapeño pepper and lime, or light fresh salads made with a beautiful combination of green and red lettuces in a piquant balsamic vinaigrette. Another excellent choice is five beans and rice; the spicy bean stew is served over a wild rice mixture that is chewy and hearty, and topped with shavings of Romano cheese. Hamburgers are overcooked, no matter how you order them—so beware. The Tap Room meat pie is not special. Great French fries are made from fresh potatoes with their skins on and are served with homemade ketchup spiced with cumin, chipotle pepper, and cinnamon and a mayonnaise based sauce with crushed green peppercorns. They serve very good cod, fried in beer batter, with fries; goat's-milk cheese rarebit; peel-and-eat shrimp; and a vegetarian sandwich made with cheese, avocado, and other vegetables on focaccia with garlic and thyme sauce.

For dessert there is deliciously rich sticky toffee pudding, a rich concoction of dense cake with caramel sauce and whipped cream. No matter what your business or pleasure in St. Louis, if you are anywhere near the downtown area, the Tap Room is a good choice for lunch or casual dinner.

Special Events

St. Louis Friends of James Beard dinners
Four times per year
8816 Manchester Rd., Box 258
St. Louis 63144
Write to them to get on the mailing list

Four times every year, the public is invited by the St. Louis Friends of James Beard to indulge in the combined culinary talents of some of the country's great chefs. St. Louisans who love food will not want to miss these events, sponsored by this young organization, which incidentally, is the first satellite of the New York-based James Beard House, the country's most important culinary arts center. The dinners provide the unique opportunity to sample the talents of not one, but many fine chefs, including those who work at area country clubs and restaurants and guest chefs from some of the best restaurants in the country. Of the four dinners, three are five-course sit-down dinners which can cost from $55 to $100, including wine. One dinner, in September, is a buffet-style family barbecue, which, at $25 per ticket for adults and $10 for children, is one of St. Louis's great culinary bargains.

The BBQ is an event that showcases local talent. At a recent BBQ, the following chefs participated: Chris Desens from the Country Club at the Legends, Lisa Slay from Blue Water Grill, Brian Stapleton from the Ritz-Carlton, John Kennealy from the Noonday Club, David Timney from Café Balaban, Brian Menzel from Boone Valley Golf Club, and Neika Soisson from Soisson's Confections. Guests were dazzled by the menu which consisted of more than 30 dishes, including main courses of barbecued Thai lamb, southern seafood sausages on herb buns, medallions of beef with wild rice pancakes and smoky corn sauce, barbecued spiced salmon, baby free-range chicken with garlic and charred tomato vinaigrette, and hamburgers and hot dogs. Vegetable dishes included champagne cucumber cocktails, grilled corn on the cob with red pepper cilantro butter, yellow tomatoes and fresh buffalo mozzarella with basil oil, grilled vegetable gazpacho, pickled peppers, and cucumber, tomato, and Gorgonzola salad. For dessert there were bourbon-pecan ice cream sandwiches, apple pie with walnut crunch ice-cream, carrot cake with heath bar icing, strawberry shortcake, and an assortment of cookies and homemade ice creams. There are only 100 tickets available for this event.

The sit-down dinners are usually for 50 to 75 people. There is typically at least one guest chef from out of town who works with four or five local chefs to create culinary magic. Sometimes these dinners include wines from a variety of vineyards and other times they showcase wines from from one particular vineyard, such as Chateau Montelena in Napa Valley. One recent sit-down dinner featured the cooking of Allen Sternweiler of Printer's Row in Chicago, Bob Vickers from the Racquet Club, John Bogacki from Westwood Country Club, Chris Desens from the Country Club at the Legends, and Neika Soisson from Soisson's Confections. Hors d'oeuvres consisted of venison tartare on sweet potato chips, wild mushroom and pheasant crisp, Jack Daniels smoked shrimp wrapped in potato, and onion and oyster pots of gold. The first course was sautéed halibut with roasted fennel broth, followed by seared tuna in green peppercorn paste on onion confit and black olive couscous, elk loin and rabbit tamale, a selection of cheeses, and plum strudel in ginger plum sauce with white chocolate-mandarin-orange grapes. These events are usually held in winter, early summer, early fall (BBQ), and late fall. They are simply not to be missed.

Teddy Bear Tea
Ritz-Carlton
100 Carondelet Plaza
Clayton 63105
(314) 863-6300

In the sumptuous lobby lounge of the Ritz-Carlton, adults indulge in traditional British-style high tea. But between Thanksgiving and Christmas, you can indulge your favorite child when teddy bears and gingerbread transform the already elegant setting into a magical childhood fantasy. A full-size gingerbread village, complete with a moving toy train, captivates kids; a piano player performs cheery holiday music; and kids and their lucky adult companions are served at tea tables with plush upholstered chairs or couches and coffee tables. Children receive a plate with finger sandwiches, a brownie, and cookies, and predictably, as if it were a rule chiseled in stone, all children go for the brownie first. Adults are treated to a two-course full tea service. The first course consists of a nice selection of delicate tea sandwiches that includes sandwiches of smoked salmon, asparagus and ham, and cucumber. A delicious scone served with Devonshire cream (that looks like whipped butter but tastes like heaven) accompanies the first course's sandwiches. The second course includes a tasty selection of sweet breads, petit fours, and tarts. For the kids there is hot chocolate, and for adults there is a choice of tea: both are unobtrusively kept hot. Children gather on the grand staircase for songs and then bring their teddy bears to hear stories in front of the marble staircase. The Teddy Bear Tea is a very special treat for children and their fortunate companions. There are two seatings on the days that Teddy Bear Tea is available, at 12:30 PM and 3:00 PM. Reservations are essential.

A Bite to Eat

If you're in the vicinity of any of these places, they are all good bets for light meals or snacks. All are inexpensive.

Café Beignet
515 S. Main
St. Charles 63301
(314) 947-3000
Open: Wednesday through Sunday,
8:30 AM–3:00 PM (Saturday and Sunday until 4:00 PM)

St. Charles is a charming old river town that caters to tourists. Typically, towns like these have lots of restaurants and few of them are good. Café Beignet is a fun place to stop for Cajun-inspired breakfast or lunch. Try Cajun stew, a spicy mixture of smoky sausage, chicken, and vegetables, that is served with salad and a moist delicious hunk of warm cornbread that has a liberal scattering of jalapeño peppers. Tender Creole chicken is rubbed in spices, grilled, and served atop spicy rice. Hearty sandwiches made on Kaiser buns can be purchased whole or half, and the restaurant has a children's menu. For dessert there are good beignets. The restaurant also has a bar and an outdoor patio for dining in good weather.

Cafeteria Almadenah
3586 Adie Rd.
St. Ann 63074
(314) 298-8586
Open: Daily, 10:00 AM–8:00 PM
(Sunday 11:00 AM–6:00 PM)

A few blocks from Northwest Plaza Shopping Center in St. Ann is this small middle-eastern restaurant that is part of the International Food and Bakery shop. The restaurant serves middle-eastern specialties from a menu and from a blackboard menu of daily specials written in Arabic. An outstanding sandwich is the shawerma, which is similar to a gyro sandwich but far superior. Made with lamb that is stacked and roasted on a vertical rotisserie and sliced thin, then piled into a split fresh pita with tomatoes, spiced onions, a slice of imported pickle, and a smooth tahini based sauce, this spicy sandwich is wonderful. You can also get meat and spinach pies, hummus (a chickpea and tahini dip), baba ghanoush (an eggplant and tahini dip), falafel (deep fried balls of ground spiced beans), and kibbe (beef, bulgar, onion, and pinenut patties) served either raw or cooked. For a full hot meal, ask about the daily specials.

Culpeppers
300 N. Euclid
St. Louis 63108
(314) 361-2828
Open: Daily, 11:00 AM–1:00 AM
(Sunday noon until midnight)

An offensive sign on the door informs you that children under 12 are not welcome, so if you're not in the presence of kids (and not offended), you might want to stop in and try Culpeppers spicy chicken wings—they're very good. The wings are crisp and smothered in a Louisiana hot sauce which is not sweet but rather has lots of vinegar and pepper to give it kick. If you ask, the heaping plate of wings is served with a creamy blue cheese dressing on the side.

Dvin-Armenian, Russian, Greek Restaurant
8143 Big Bend
Webster Groves 63119
(314) 968-4000
Open: Daily, 11:30 AM–8:30 PM
(Friday and Saturday until 9:30 and Sunday noon–5:00 PM)

When looking for an unusual lunch in Webster Groves, stop at this small storefront restaurant for beef Armenian style. This hearty stew of beef, onions, and dried fruit including apricots, prunes, and raisins is quite good served as a sandwich on warm pita and sprinkled with ruby-red pomegranate seeds. The sandwich is served with a salad of mostly lettuce with shredded feta cheese and a piquant vinaigrette. Unfortunately, other items on the menu are not particularly good, but the tasty stew makes a good lunch.

Gus' Pretzel Shop
1820 Arsenal
St. Louis 63118
(314) 664-4010
Open: Tuesday through Sunday, 7:00 AM–4:00 PM
(Sunday until 2:00 PM)

When near the Anheuser-Busch brewery during lunch, stop in at Gus's, a small shop that has been turning out hand-twisted soft pretzels since 1920 for a unique treat: Gus's pretzel sandwich. This is a take out lunch—there is nowhere to eat in the small shop. You have your choice of either bratwurst or salsiccia sausage wrapped in a pretzel stick, which is baked to a glossy golden brown. This combination really works: the salsiccia is juicy and just spicy enough and the pretzel is crunchy on the outside and soft on the inside.

Mediterranean Express
6655 Delmar (in the University City
Market in the Loop)
University City 63130
(314) 721-6474
Open: Daily, 11:00 AM–8:00 PM
(Sunday noon–5:00 PM)

When shopping at the University City Loop Produce Market, stop at the Mediterranean Express for a crisp, freshly fried falafel (ground beans and spices shaped into balls and deep fried) wrapped in warm pita, with lettuce, tomato, onion, spices, and topped with a creamy hummus-based sauce. You can sit at one of the tables in the atrium of the Market in the Loop and eat or take it on your way.

Schatz's Deli and Pizza
110 N. Clay Ave.
Kirkwood 63122
(314) 821-7447
Open: Monday through Saturday,
11:00 AM–6:00 PM (Saturday 11:00 AM–3:00 PM)

This small deli in Kirkwood is a good place to stop for a veggie sandwich—a unique sandwich of marinated artichoke hearts paired with pepper cheese and topped with fresh slices of pepper, tomato, red onion, and sprouts, with a sweet vinaigrette. It is served on herb bread and makes a tasty and unusual lunch. Hot daily specials are also available.

Winery of the Little Hills
501 S. Main St.
St. Charles 63301
(314) 946-9339
Open: Daily 10:00 AM –6:00 PM (Sunday from noon) and until
11:00 PM on summer weekends

If you find yourself in St. Charles during outdoor season and you have a bit of time to relax, stop at this wine bar for a sample of Missouri wines. Try the Norton or Cynthiana—both are good red wines—and then go into the beautiful terraced garden and drink wine and watch the world go by. You can enjoy a bite of cheese with your wine. The winery carries the delicious raw milk cheeses of Morningland Dairy. Try the sharp cheddar.

Woofie's
1919 Woodson Rd.
Overland 63114
(314) 426-6291
Open: Daily 10:30 AM–10:00 PM (Sunday 11:30 AM–7:00 PM)

When you drive up to this hot dog stand to eat at the counter or take out your dog, don't be surprised to see BMWs parked next to pick-up trucks in the lot. Woofie's is that kind of place. The hot dogs are good for three reasons: they are all-beef Vienna dogs in casing that gives them snap when you bite into them, they are not overcooked, and they are served in poppy seed buns with the right kind of condiments. The crisp, thin fries are served with seasoned salt. Woofies also serves hamburgers, pastrami, sausages, tamales, and their variations.

Specialty Food Shops

Asia Market
2234 S. Brentwood
Brentwood 63144
(314) 962-6778
Open: Daily, 10:00 AM–8:00 PM
(Sunday 11:30 AM–6:00 PM)

This Asian specialty market is well stocked with canned goods, fresh produce, and some frozen prepared foods. It has a variety of oils, soy sauces, teas, noodles, dried fish, fish sauces, dried seaweeds, and huge bags of rice hailing from such countries as Korea, the Philippines, Indonesia, Thailand, China, Taiwan, and Japan. Fresh produce includes seasonal selections such as apples, persimmons, chestnuts, and other items such as taro root, hot and sweet peppers, chrysanthemum, and ginger. Refrigerated cases stock shrimp and fish, tofu, kimchi, nuts, and pickles. There are frozen noodles, meats, and rice cakes. The shop also has cooking utensils, dolls, knickknacks, videotapes, and cosmetics.

Athenian Greek Imports
7006 Clayton Rd.
Richmond Heights 63117
(314) 645-7337
Open: Daily 10:00 AM–5:00 PM
(Sunday noon–3:00 PM)

This wonderful, narrow little shop sells everything you need for an authentic Greek feast. It has an array of imported Greek specialty foods including cheeses, olives, spices, grains, beans, oils, jams, fruits, and sweets. It also has a selection of excellent homemade items that you can eat at one of the few tables in the front of the shop or take home for dinner or a dinner party. Try the *spanakopita* (cheese-spinach pie) or the *tiropita* (cheese pie), both of which have an interesting mixture of Greek cheeses in a flaky phyllo pastry. There are appetizers with such tantalizing combinations of ingredients as cheese, mushrooms, nuts, and wild rice in phyllo dough; beef sausage, wild rice, and currants wrapped in phyllo; and vine leaves stuffed with rice, pinenuts, and currants. Entrees include such well-known Greek favorites as moussaka, the layered eggplant dish, and pasticho, the layered macaroni, lamb, and cheese dish. Both are delicious, each with its own unique blend of spices. There are gyros and shish kabobs. Homemade Greek pastries run the gamut from the heavy and intensely sweet baklava, to a light, delicate butter cookie flavored with ouzo and topped with powdered sugar, to those made with crunchy nuts or sesame seeds. The shop has a small but good selection of cheeses such as tangy feta, sharp kasseri, smooth sheep's-milk manouri, and fun-for-the-kids string cheese.

Becker's
3183 South Grand
St. Louis 63118
(314) 771-7432
Open: Tuesday through Saturday,
10:00 AM–5:00 PM

St. Louis's Italian community has the Hill. The rest of the European community has more geographically dispersed shops in which to find foods from "home." The shelves in this old-world shop are crammed with canned goods and jars laden with fruits, vegetables, jams, pickles, and mustards, as well as imported gifts. A meat counter features about 15 types of meats. Another counter has a small selection of cheeses, mostly imported from Denmark, Holland, Switzerland, and France. German rye breads, one of which has the shape and heft of a brick, are for sale. The shop has some imported wines and liquors, as well as beautiful gifts including Blue Delft porcelain, fancy steins from Germany, and crystal from Russia. Dolls, record albums, cookbooks, and moose horns are some of the other items stuffing the shelves at Becker's.

V. Bommarito Wines and Food
8137 Maryland Ave.
Clayton 63105
(314) 863-4090
Open: Monday through Saturday,
10:00 AM–6:00 PM

This small, elegant shop specializes in Italian wines and foods. Although the emphasis is on Italian wines, you also can find a limited selection of California wines and a small selection of quality French wines, that includes some older vintages. In addition to the wines, you will find fine estate-bottled olive oils and balsamic vinegars, specialty pastas, Arborio rice, dried porcini mushrooms, a few Italian cheeses, imported jars of fruit and jams, and other select items. If you get there at the right time of day, you can buy a delicious loaf of ciabatta, the house bread of Tony's restaurant. The semi-flat loaf of crusty rustic peasant bread is baked on the premises daily. On Saturdays, there are wine tastings.

Brandt's Market and Café
6525 Delmar
University City 63130
(314) 727-3663
Open: Daily 8:30 AM–10:00 PM (Friday and
Saturday until midnight and Sunday 9:30 AM–10:00 PM)

Brandt's is a unique specialty foods shop that, over the years, has evolved into a hybrid natural foods-gourmet specialty shop, beer and wine shop, and coffeehouse-restaurant. It seems to be constantly nudging its customers to expand their culinary experiences by bringing in new products for them to try. Brandt's carries organic produce, a small selection of imported cheeses, and bulk foods such as dried fruits, nuts, pastas, beans, granolas, snack foods, grains, and rices. You can stop in to buy a loaf of bread from Companion Baking Company, which bakes such incredible breads as pine nut-fig bread. Brandt's has spices, sauces, mustards, vinegars, jams, salsas, oils, grind-it-yourself peanut butter, and all of the other natural and gourmet foods you expect to find. It has teas and vacuum packed coffees, as well as tea pots and coffee pots. Brandt's has an impressive selection of domestic and imported beers. It is also a good place to go for a last minute dinner wine because, although the selection is small, it is a good one. Brandt's is kind of a local cultural institution which keeps late hours, presents live music, and has tables where you can have a light meal or a cup of cappuccino and a pastry from among the city's best bakeries.

The Cheese Place
9755 Manchester Rd.
Rock Hill 63119
(314) 962-8150
Open: Monday through Saturday, 9:00 AM–7:00 PM
Another location in: Chesterfield, (314) 227-9001

Cheese lovers, beware of heart palpitations; this shop is cheese nirvana. It has more than 200 varieties of imported and domestic cheeses, hailing from 18 countries. The Cheese Place is much more than a cheese store, but more about that later. At the cheese counter, knowledgeable staff will cheerfully encourage you to sample a variety of cheeses. Let your palate experience the difference between the intensely sharp flavor of Gorgonzola naturale and the sweet lively flavor of Gorgonzola verde dolce, and compare those to the flavors of ten or so other blue cheeses. Find out why the Argentinean version of Reggiano Parmesan can't stand up to the subtly nutty flavor of the real thing. There are goat's-milk cheeses, sheep's-milk cheeses, and even buffalo's-milk cheeses, in addition to cow's-milk cheeses. You can try fresh cheese, aged cheese, very aged cheese, and cheese that has been kneaded and shaped. At the Cheese Place, you will find not just soft creamy goat's-milk cheese like Montrachet, but a variety of goat's-milk cheeses, such as Cabrales, a semi-hard cheese from Spain. Don't miss the opportunity to sample hard-to-find Taleggio, the rich soft-ripened cheese from

Italy, or the unusual gjetost, a Norwegian cheese made from milk whey (rather than curds) that has a fudgelike consistency and slightly sweet flavor. When you've finally made your cheese selection, you can buy the bread to spread it on; the Cheese Store carries the excellent breads of La Bonne Bouchée, Pan Dora, and Companion Baking Company. And, you can complement your purchases with wine. The Cheese Place has one of St. Louis's most comprehensive selections of wine, with a strong emphasis on wines from California and France.

In addition to cheese and its necessary complements, this store carries excellent coffees and nuts that are fresh roasted on the premises. These coffees and nuts, as well as dried fruits, chocolate and hard candies are sold in bulk so that you can purchase exactly the quantity you need. Serious bakers can find such fine European baking chocolates as Callebaut in an 11 pound money-saving bar. The store has a good selection of European chocolate bars, as well as other specialty foods. It has a deli counter with specialty meats, pâtés and mousses, and olives. It has a freezer stocked with pastas stuffed with the likes of porcini mushrooms or Gorgonzola cheese. It carries a selection of dried wild mushrooms. The Cheese Place is one of St. Louis's most important gourmet food and wine shops.

East East Oriental Grocery
8619 Olive St. Rd.
University City 63132
(314) 432-5590
Open: Daily 10:30 AM–8:00 PM
(Sunday 11:30 AM–6:00 PM)

This bright shop has a large selection of Asian foods, with a strong emphasis on foods from Korea. There is a good selection of fresh produce, frozen fish and noodles, and tofu that you can buy in bulk. The shelves are well stocked with a such items as oils, sauces, teas, noodles, spices, canned fruits, dried seaweeds, dried mushrooms, and huge bags of rice. There are some frozen and refrigerated prepared foods and a variety of cooking utensils.

Golden Grocer
335 N. Euclid
St. Louis 63108
(314) 367-0405
Open: Daily 10:00 AM–7:00 PM
(Sunday noon–5:00 PM)

The Golden Grocer is a large natural and gourmet food market. It has a good selection of organic produce, a refrigerated section with cheeses, yogurts, and other fresh foods, and a freezer stocked with entrees and other frozen items. It has a large section of bulk items including herbs and spices, nuts, grains, rice, beans, and dried fruits. You also can buy oils, honey, tamari, and liquid soap in bulk at the Golden Grocer. It carries cookies, crackers, snack foods, cereals, jams, nut butters, pastas, juices, and teas. It carries diet supplements, books, cleaning supplies, natural cosmetics, and even pet food.

Gourmet to Go
7807 Clayton Rd.
Clayton 63117
(314) 727-2442
Open: Monday through Saturday,
10:00 AM–7:00 PM
Another location at: 9828 Clayton Rd.,
Ladue (314) 993-5442

Gourmet to Go is the answer for busy people who enjoy good food but don't have time to prepare it and don't care much about cost. The two retail shops always have an excellent selection of fresh salads, soups, appetizers, entrées, and desserts from which to choose for your last-minute take-out dinner or spontaneous get together. But a large menu is available from which you can order in advance for your office meeting, picnic, or party. So if you're in the mood for Boursin chicken, boneless stuffed quail, or beef tenderloin with bordelaise sauce, give them a call and they will deliver it or have it ready for you to pick up.

Japanese Food Imports
1051 S. Big Bend
Richmond Heights 63117
(314) 644-3004
Open: Tuesday through Sunday,
10:00 AM–6:00 PM (Sunday from 1:00 PM)

This tidy Japanese market carries a large selection of Japanese foods, from traditional foods to imported junk food. Look in the refrigerator case for fresh noodles, fresh seaweed, pickled ginger and vegetables, miso, tofu, and cooked shrimp powder. A freezer case holds such delectables as dumplings, noodles, vegetables, prepared foods, sausages, and fermented beans. The shelves are stacked with a variety of sauces, oils, vinegars, wines, teas, soup mixes, dried seaweeds, spices, dried noodles, rice flour, and canned fruits and vegetables such as lychees, boiled taros, and bamboo shoots. Large bags of rice are stacked up neatly in the front of the store. On Thursday, Friday, and Saturday, the market carries five of six types of fresh fish for making sashimi or sushi. You can buy royal jelly or bee pollen if you are inclined, as well as origami supplies, a small selection of cooking and eating utensils, and tea and sake sets.

Jay's International Food Co.
3172 South Grand
St. Louis 63118
(314) 772-2552
Open: Daily, 9:00 AM–8:00 PM
(Sunday until 7:00 PM)

Although there is a strong emphasis on Asian and East Indian imported foods, Mexico, Jamaica, and numerous other countries all have their space at this truly international market. The enticing scents of spices and pungent dried fish fill the air. Huge burlap bags of rice from a variety of sources are stacked in the window. On a given day in Jay's produce section, you might find such items as fresh bamboo shoots, sugar cane, tiny round green eggplants, chiles, broccoli rabe, tomatillos, yams and tubers of various origins, bananas in all sizes and states of ripeness, persimmons, mangoes, papayas, coconuts, and wonderful fresh herbs such as Thai basil, dill, cilantro, lemon grass, and watercress that are often available even in the dead of winter. Shelves are stacked with dried hot peppers and spices that you can purchase in bulk or that are mixed in combinations in the forms of curries and Jamaican jerks. Noodles in a variety of styles, from rice to transparent, are available. Bulk beans, rice, and nuts are for sale. Cans, jars, and bottles are filled with a dizzying selection of soy sauces, oils, fish pastes, chili sauces, bean sauces, and pastes to suit even the pickiest recipe. A fresh meat counter features livers, hocks, ribs, hearts, and kidneys, along with more common cuts, and live blue crabs slowly move about enticing young children. You can find Chihuahua cheese from Mexico, tofu, and other dairy products in the dairy section. At Jay's you can buy not only authentic ingredients but also the tools you will need to cook: woks in a variety of sizes, rice cookers, utensils, and serving dishes are available.

Mangia Italiano
3145 South Grand
St. Louis 63118
(314) 664-8585
Open: Monday through Friday
11:00 AM–9:00 PM

Funky, outrageous, and fun—Mangia Italiano is a fresh pasta shop that has evolved into a restaurant and coffeehouse. If fresh pasta is your passion, Mangia Italiano turns out 144 varieties of fresh pasta—some in very unusual flavors. These are hearty and chewy, rather than fine and silky pastas. Some of the flavors that are available are squid ink (which is black), red pepper, spinach, jalapeño, onion, chipolte, whole wheat, orange-cinnamon, and tomato. They come in a variety of shapes ranging from shells to long strands, to stuffed agnolotti (ravioli-like pasta with cheese filling that includes the wonderful sharp flavor of pecorino Romano).

Maria and Son
4201 Hereford at Chippewa
St. Louis 63109
(314) 481-9009
Open: Monday through Saturday,
8:00 AM–5:00 PM (Saturday 9:00 AM–2:00 PM)

Maria and Son popularized the famous St. Louis specialty, breaded ravioli, which is commonly served with Parmesan cheese or sauce as an appetizer. The company also produces other good frozen pastas. A great deal of the pasta that is served in Italian restaurants in St. Louis comes from Maria and Son. Although these frozen pastas can be purchased in grocery stores throughout St. Louis, smart shoppers will want to know that these products are much cheaper when purchased at the Maria and Son shop. The breaded ravioli are tender and tasty if they are properly deep fried. Kids love them! Especially good are the spinach tortellini filled with meat. They can be purchased in money-saving five-pound bags. Also available are cheese or meat ravioli, cannelloni, lasagna, and gnocchi. Any of these pastas can be served with your own sauce, but Maria and Son has frozen sauces available.

Mound City Shelled Nut Co.
7831 Olive St.
University City 63130
(314) 725-9040
Open: Monday through Friday,
9:00 AM–4:30 PM

The nuts are fresh—they roast them on the premises—at this shop which happens to be kosher. Here you can buy almonds, Brazil nuts, cashews, filberts (hazelnuts), macadamias, peanuts, pecans, pine nuts, pistachios, and walnuts (black or English), as well as sunflower, pumpkin, sesame, poppy, and squash seeds. You can buy some of the nuts raw as well as roasted. Mound City also carries a few dried fruits including apricots, figs, and crystallized ginger, and a selection of bulk hard candies including salt-free and sugar-free candies.

Natural Way
8110 Big Bend Blvd.
Webster Groves 63119
(314) 961-3541
Open: Daily 9:30 AM–8:00 PM
(Saturday until 6:30 PM and Sunday noon–5:00 PM)
Another location at: 12345 Olive St. Rd.,
Creve Coeur (314) 878-3001 (call for hours)

Natural Way is a wonderful bright and cheerful health food market with a good selection of organic produce; a frozen foods section carrying mostly prepared entrées, desserts, and breads; and a refrigerated section with cheeses, cheese substitutes, milk, and yogurts. It has a large section of bulk items including herbs and spices, nuts, granolas, candies, grains, rice, beans, and dried fruits. Natural Way carries fresh Great Harvest breads. There is organic baby food, pet food, cookies, crackers, snack foods, cereals, grind-your-own peanut butter, jams, nut butters, pastas, juices, and teas. The market also carries diet supplements, books, cleaning supplies, natural cosmetics, and even bee pollen. A refrigerated take-out counter offers freshly made salads and soups. The market has another small location in Creve Coeur.

Protzel's Delicatessen
7608 Wydown
Clayton 63105
(314) 721-4445
Open: Tuesday through Sunday,
7:30 AM–5:30 PM (Sunday until 3:00 PM)

The corned beef is very good—cooked fresh daily—at this neighborhood deli that has been serving customers for more than 40 years. It is a good place to stop when you haven't the vaguest idea what to serve for dinner. There are no tables at this take-out deli. They make their own knishes at Protzel's, and although it seems a contradiction to describe a knish as "light," when they are fresh, Protzel's knishes do not sink in your stomach like lead balloons. The dough is flaky and the potato knish, which is made the old-fashioned (and pre-cholesterol-conscious) way with schmaltz, is a treat. Some of the other sandwiches served at the deli are rare roast beef, pastrami, peppered beef, turkey, tongue, salami (both regular and hard), chopped liver, lox and cream cheese, and various combination sandwiches. A large slice of dill pickle accompanies each sandwich. You also can buy homemade frozen or fresh-to-order items such as kasha, kishka, kugel, hot brisket in gravy, blintzes, stuffed cabbage, and chicken soup with matzo balls or kreplach. Call for availability of these items.

River City Nutrition
112 E. Jefferson
Kirkwood 63122
(314) 822-1406
Open: Daily 9:00 AM–6:30 PM
(Saturday until 5:30 PM and Sunday noon–5:00 PM)
Other locations in: Florrisant, Chesterfield, and Alton

River City Nutrition has all the foods you'd expect to find in a health food store. Organic produce, a large selection of bulk pastas, beans, granolas, rices, grains, nuts, snack foods, spices and more. It has organic baby foods, cereals, nut butters, honey, juices, and a variety of sugars such as date sugar, maple sugar, and turbinado sugar. A refrigerated section features yogurts, cheeses, nuts, and lunch meats.

The Roasting House
11034 Olive St. Rd.
Creve Coeur 63141
(314) 432-5577
Open: Monday through Saturday,
9:00 AM–7:00 PM

Called the Roasting House because it sells nuts and coffees that are freshly roasted on the premises of its sister shop, the Cheese Place, this specialty shop sells in bulk, which allows you to get exactly the amount you need of such items as freshly roasted pecans, pine nuts, almonds, cashews, hazelnuts, and pistachios. There are two dozen or so dried fruit varieties including dried cranberries, blueberries, cherries, kiwis, mangoes, apricots, dates, nectarines, papayas, and currants. The bulk section includes an unusual and interesting selection of chocolates such as six varieties of chocolate-covered almonds including gold wrapped almonds; dark chocolate cordials; chocolate-covered dried cherries, orange peel, and ginger; and chocolate-covered espresso beans. Sugar-free hard candies and chocolate candies are also sold in bulk. The shop has a large variety of coffees, including flavored coffees, that you can purchase ground or as beans. A deli counter has imported cheeses, specialty meats, and pâtés and terrines. In addition to the bulk items, there are gourmet specialty items such as oils, pastas, and sauces. The shop carries a good selection of wine. The Roasting House is a great place to select a unique and delicious gift.

Seema Enterprises
10618 Page
Overland 63132
(314) 423-9990
Open: Daily, 9:00 AM–8:00 PM (Saturday
from 10:00 AM and Sunday 11:00 AM–5:00 PM)
Another location at: 52 Manchester Mall,
Manchester (314) 391-5914 (call for hours)

Follow the aroma, and you will be in the food section of this enticing shop that features the specialties of India and Pakistan. Lentils, beans, nuts, seeds, and oils such as jasmine, almond, olive, mustard, and sesame are available. The store carries more than ten varieties of flour such as rice flour, *masa harina, moong* flour, *nirav besan,* and *dokra* flour. You can buy your spices individually or already mixed and sold as curry powders. Various chutneys, pickles, and canned fruits line the shelves. A nice selection of fresh produce is on hand that most likely will include various root spices, cilantro, peppers, and seasonal vegetables such as eggplant and a specialty okra. Drinks include teas, juices, and syrups. There are breads and snack foods and a refrigerator case stocks sweets from a bakery in New York as well as prepared entrees.

Stack's Fine Cheese
6655 Delmar (in the University City
Market in the Loop)
University City 63130
(314) 725-9490
Open: Tuesday through Saturday,
9:30 AM–6:00 PM

This small shop in the University City Market in the Loop carries a selection of 50 or so cheeses, about half of which are domestic. Look for hard-to-find fresh mozzarella and goat's milk cheese here. The shop also has imported olives and some deli meats, as well as smoked chickens, slab bacon, and sausages from Washington, Missouri.

Starr's
1135 S. Big Bend
Richmond Heights 63117
(314) 781-2345
Open: Monday through Saturday,
9:00 AM–7:00 PM

Starr's is a large gourmet market that sells fresh organic produce, baked goods, wonderfully fresh fish, free-range chickens and eggs, some meat, freshly roasted coffee, and lots of wine. It has a deli counter with salads, meats, cheeses, and pâtés. Its shelves are stocked with specialty foods including sauces, spices, pastas, rices, chocolates, and a selection of health foods. The shop has bulk foods including dried fruits, beans, nuts, lentils, flours, granolas, and more. A smoker provides the shop with delicious cold-smoked Scottish-style salmon, smoked trout, and smoked chicken.

One of the best reasons to shop at Starr's is the coffee. There are fourteen blends and varietals that are fresh roasted on the premises and the prices are substantially less than the competition. Starr's has one of the area's largest selections of wine, from the inexpensive to the very expensive. From time to time Starr's has wine tastings and on weekends there are wines available in the store for tasting.

Tong's Special Foods
10571 Old Olive St. Rd.
Creve Coeur 63141
(314) 997-0540
Open: Monday through Saturday,
9:00 AM–6:00 PM

This large, bright new location for Tong's carries on the shop's tradition as the oldest health food store in St. Louis. It has a large selection of health and special diet foods, including kosher foods. Look for prepackaged (no bulk items) beans, rices, cereals, pastas, spices, and nuts. Lots of sweeteners, such as maple syrup, molasses, turbinado sugar, and honey, share shelf space with nut butters, baby foods, cookies, and snack foods. There are teas, coffees, and juices. Tong's has a refrigerated case with such items as cheeses, eggs, and tofu and a frozen section with ice cream and ice cream substitutes and entrees. It has books, supplements, and cosmetics. Tong's does not carry fresh produce.

Tropicana Market
5001 Lindenwood at Hereford
St. Louis 63109
(314) 353-7328 and (800) 397-0228
Open: Daily 9:00 AM–9:00 PM and
Sunday 11:00 AM–5:00 PM

You can almost feel the hot tropical sun at this market that carries the foods of Spain, Latin America, and the West Indies. Stop at the fresh produce counter and perhaps find cactus flowers, epazote, green coconuts, sugar cane, yuca, jalapeños, or baby bananas. Move on to the frozen food section to find tamales, tripe, burritos, and banana leaves. You can find cheeses from Mexico, Spain, and elsewhere. A selection of canned fish and seafood, two-dozen-or-so varieties of chili peppers and other spices, olive oils, olives, cans of tropical juices, and rice all compete for shelf space. Tropicana has fresh flour and corn tortillas, as well as locally baked guava and mango muffins. Candies and syrups made from boiled-down condensed milk and sugar, sweet potatoes boiled in sugar until they are solid enough to be candy, and guava paste that is served layered with a cream-style cheese, are some of the wonderful, authentic sweets you can find at Tropicana. A good selection of Mexican beers is also available.

Viviano and Sons, Importers of Italian Foods
5139 Shaw
St. Louis 63110
(314) 771-5476
Open: Monday through Saturday,
8:00 AM–5:00 PM

Viviano's is the quintessential Italian grocery. A mainstay of the Hill for more than 40 years, people searching for authentic Italian groceries (as well as an authentic Italian shopping experience), know they can find what they want at Viviano's. This grocery devotes an entire shelf to imported pastas in a dizzying selection. Other shelves are crammed with the makings of fine Italian cuisine: olive oils in a large selection of qualities and quantities, balsamic vinegars in an equally impressive selection, canned tomatoes, sun-dried tomatoes, capers, artichokes, anchovies, imported tuna fish, and olives. You can buy prepared sauces such as marinara, pesto, and clam. Bulk items including hard-to-find lupini and fava beans; nuts including pistachios, with or without shells, and pine nuts, pecans, hazelnuts, and almonds; spices and herbs; dried porcini mushrooms; and dried fruits are available. Unusual items such as grapeseed oil, hazelnut oil, and olive oil soap have their places on the shelves. A deli counter with enormous wheels of imported Italian cheeses including Romano, Reggiano Parmesan, and Asiago, give the shop a delicious aroma, and the counter also sells meats such as prosciutto, mortadella, and salami, a good selection of olives and olive salads, sardines in salt brine, and other delicacies.

You can find fresh pizza dough and a variety of fresh and grated cheeses at the refrigerated section of the shop. Freezers stock fresh frozen pasta including tortellini, ravioli, gnocchi, and cannelloni. Looking for dried and salted fish? Viviano's carries them. Be sure to stop at the fresh produce section. Sometimes the counter has nothing but wilted vegetables, but at other times you can find fresh figs, cactus pears, and fresh olives that you can cure yourself with the help of a recipe that is posted on the counter. The shop has items for baking such as imported chocolates, chestnuts, and almond paste. It has a wonderful selection of imported Italian cooking utensils and gadgets. Viviano's carries breads and imported cookies. But the Italian loaf is better at Amighetti's (on the Hill) and why buy cookies that have been sitting on the shelf for who knows how long, when you can walk a few blocks to the Missouri Baking Co. for great baked-today cookies?

Wine Merchant
20 S. Hanley Rd.
(314) 863-6282
Clayton 63105
Open: Monday through Saturday,
10:00 AM–8:00 PM

The temperature-controlled Wine Merchant is a wonderful place to shop for wine. Its huge selection includes wines from California, France (with a strong selection of red and white Burgundies), Italy, Germany, and elsewhere. The wines are well organized, the aisles spacious, and the salespeople are helpful. The shop carries a large selection of wine including half-bottles, magnums, double magnums and even a nine-liter bottle (a case of wine in a bottle!). They sell a large selection of imported beers, and a small selection of imported cheeses and specialty food items. On Saturdays, featured wines are available for sampling.

Chocolates and Ice Cream

Andre's Swiss Confiserie
1026 S. Brentwood Blvd.
Richmond Heights 63117
(314) 727-9928
Open: Monday through Saturday,
7:00 AM–5:30 PM (Friday until 9:00 PM)
Another location at: 16 N. Central, Clayton
(314) 727-0016 (call for hours)

Is it a bakery or a candy shop? Or a restaurant? In his native Switzerland, Andre's owner Ulrich Wagner was trained as a confiseur, which means he trained in the art of making pastries and confections. His shop is a confiserie—a tea room, which serves pastries and lunches with a distinctive northern European bent. And while European definitions of what is a bakery and what is a confectionery might be rigid, here in St. Louis, one thing is clear: when in the vicinity of Galleria, don't miss the opportunity to buy a selection of traditional European-style pastries and chocolates.

Andre's style is northern European with chocolate and nuts playing the central role. The chocolate is wonderful—rich and silky smooth. The nuts, primarily almond, are combined in pastries and chocolates or sculpted into fruits or other whimsical marzipans. Mediterranean pistachio nuts and hazelnuts have found their way into Andre's confections. In fact, some of the very best selections are made with finely ground hazelnuts combined with silky smooth chocolate into rich tender morsels. Try the Angelica, a layered confection of light and dark chocolate and finely ground hazelnuts. Or try any of the variety of rich truffles. You can mix your own selection of chocolates or buy a box already mixed—they make wonderful gifts. A selection of pastries might include tarts of almonds, apricots, and raspberry, or lemon cream and lemon custard, or rich dense chocolate truffle cream with pistachio glaze. Slices of layered pastries with mocha buttercream and cake, or apricot, almond and rum, or pastry balls filled with cake, custard, almond, and raspberry are also available to tempt you. You can buy whole cakes such as the classic Dobos torte or buttercream tortes in a variety of flavors. Andre's is open early so you can stop there and pick up delicious scones or hazelnut-filled puff pastries on your way to the office for a special treat.

During the holiday season, Andre's is a sight to behold. Chocolate-covered gingerbread houses (that stay moist and edible), chocolate wine bottles stuffed with chocolates and other artistic delectables make wonderful gifts. For the home baker and chocolate maker, Andre's stocks a large selection of fine European chocolate bars and bulk chocolates.

Bissinger French Confections
4742 McPherson Ave.
St. Louis 63198
(314) 534-2400
Open: Monday through Saturday,
9:00 AM–5:00 PM
Other locations in: Saint Louis Galleria, Plaza
Frontenac, Crestwood Plaza (call the
McPherson Ave. phone for hours)

The Bissinger family can trace its chocolate-making credentials back 300 years to 17th-century France, but its proudest achievement was receiving the patent of Confiseur Imperial from Emperor Napoleon III. It can also be proud of its contribution to St. Louis's culinary history. Since 1926, Bissinger's has been producing exquisite chocolates that combine European skill and style with some uniquely American innovations. One such innovation created and popularized by Bissinger's is the molasses caramel lollipop, made with rich molasses caramel covered in silky smooth chocolate. A chocolate molasses puff, made with crunchy spun molasses, is another molasses treat. Hawiian macadamia nuts with caramel and chocolate; heavenly hash bark; and chocolate pizza made with chocolate, pecans, and coconut are other inventive confections.

The chocolate-covered fresh raspberries at Bissinger's are divine. Unlike other chocolate-covered fruits, these large raspberries in juice are completely enrobed in chocolate. They are available in July, beginning after the fourth of July. Chocolate-dipped strawberries are another delicious seasonal treat, available Easter through September. Some of the more traditional European-style chocolates made at Bissinger's are opera cremes, truffles, marzipan, raspberry cremes, and English toffee. You can buy them already boxed or you can choose your assortment. Chocolate roses covered in red foil and chocolate hearts for Valentines Day, French marshmallow chicks, chocolate Easter bunnies, gold-foil wrapped coins (*gelt*) for Hanukkah, and shaped marzipan for Christmas make welcome traditional holiday gifts. Bissinger's chocolates can be mail-ordered. Look in the mail-order section of this book for catalog information.

Crown Candy Kitchen
1401 St. Louis Ave.
St. Louis 63106
(314) 621-9650
Open: Daily, 10:30 AM–9:00 PM
(Friday and Saturday until 10:00 PM
and Sunday noon–9:00 PM)

For more than 80 years, Crown Candy Kitchen has been scooping up homemade ice cream from its original soda bar and creating old-style candy favorites such as vanilla taffy, pecan clusters, chocolate cremes, and chocolates molded into seasonal shapes. Although nostalgia is an important ingredient at Crown, the malts, shakes, and sodas are top notch, and if the juke box playing "Shake, Rattle, and Roll" and old Chuck Berry tunes enhances the experience, so be it. You can really taste the malt in the malts and they have that wonderful teeth-tingling icy texture because they are made in metal containers that hold the cold better than do their modern-day paper counterparts. They are served in large soda glasses accompanied by the metal container which contains enough for a second person. Shakes, sodas, and sundaes, made with one of the dozen or so flavors made at Crown, round out the ice-cream menu. The shop also has a selection of sandwiches.

Merb's Candies
4000 South Grand
St. Louis 63118
(314) 832-7117
Open: Monday through Saturday,
8:30 AM–5:30 PM (Saturday until 5:00 PM)
Other locations at: 11644 Concord Village (314) 843-7118
and 15303 Manchester Rd., (314) 230-9798 (call for hours)

Merb's is a nostalgic neighborhood chocolate shop, but its fabled bionic apple is eagerly awaited throughout the St. Louis area each fall. The gigantic Jonathan apple, with its touch of tartness, makes the perfect foil for the creamy buttery-rich caramel that enrobes it. Pedestrian peanuts will not do on these apples; Instead they are rolled in chopped pecans. Or, if you prefer, no nuts at all. Merb's dips other fruits as well. Large strawberries are encased in a thick coat of chocolate, and delicious glazed Australian apricots peek out from their chocolate coat. They make their own marshmallow at Merb's, and it is mixed with coconut and chocolate in a tasty concoction called a twiggy. The chocolate-covered molasses puffs are crunchy and light and have the delicious full-flavor of molasses. There are cashew clusters, caramel, coconut brittle, caramel-pecan apricots, and chocolates molded into every shape you can think of. There are vanilla cremes, pineapple cremes, chocolate cremes, caramels, nougats, fudge, and more. Merb's chocolates are not as delicate or refined as the costlier European-style chocolates, but the offerings at Merb's are a tempting alternative.

Soisson's Confections
(314) 839-2912

Neika Soisson is an award-winning chocolatier who creates custom chocolate art. Her unique designs grace the tables at weddings and private parties and are used as both centerpieces and individual servings. She also sells a private line of truffles and individual miniatures. Trained in fine art, Soisson will work with you to create a custom chocolate sculpture, a cocoa painting, or a traditional chocolate dessert for any occasion. Call her for a consultation.

Ted Drewes Frozen Custard
6726 Chippewa St.
St. Louis 63109
(314) 481-2652
Open: Daily, 11:00 AM–11:00 PM
(closed from mid-January to mid-February)
Another location at: 4224 South Grand
(314) 352-7376 (call for hours)

As astonishing as it may seem to St. Louisans, there are people who have not heard of Ted Drewes Frozen Custard. Newcomers and people who visit St. Louis regularly for cultural events, shopping, or business might not be privy to the wonders of Ted Drewes Frozen Custard. Everyone else, it seems, is. And for good reason. The frozen custard is top notch, the service is quick and friendly, the summertime crowds are an amazing spectacle, and delicious new custard concoctions are continually being added to the menu. In addition, stories abound about Ted Drewes being offered big-dollar deals to franchise his product, and Mr. Drewes respectfully declining, thereby ensuring that Ted Drewes Frozen Custard remains a secure St. Louis treasure and Mr. Drewes himself a local folk hero.

Ted Drewes, Sr., first sold his frozen custard, made with all dairy products and fresh eggs, in 1929 at a traveling carnival. The product was so successful that he opened his first shop on

Natural Bridge Rd. the same year. In 1931, he opened the shop on Grand Ave., and it was followed in 1941 by the Chippewa shop. It was during the mid-1950s that Ted Drewes, Jr., introduced the concrete—a wonderful concoction of frozen custard with additions of fruit, nuts, and chocolate in various combinations that is so thick you can turn it upside down without spilling a drop. Today, you can choose from some 30 custard mixtures already devised, or create your own. All of the custard that comes out of the machines is vanilla, so your flavor is added when you order it. Perhaps this is one reason the quality is so good—nuts stay crunchy and fruit is not frozen too hard. Some of the wonderful flavors of concretes or sundaes are the terramizzou, made with lots of fresh pistachios and chocolate; the fox treat, made with hot fudge, raspberries, and macadamia nuts; and the cardinal sin made with tart cherries and hot fudge. They also have simple cones, dipped cones, sodas, and floats. Although you can buy the product in some supermarkets and specialty shops, don't judge it by what you can buy in a grocery; once it is frozen solid for shipping and storing, it loses some of its appeal. Besides, a drive to Ted Drewes is a great adventure for a family, a date, or out-of-town-guests.

Note: The Cheese Place carries a large selection of good quality chocolates, and chocolate covered nuts and fruit that you can buy in bulk. The shop also has a good selection of European chocolate bars and baking and candymaking chocolate for the home cook. See the Cheese Place in this section of the book for more information.

Cookware Shops

Abbey's Apron String
2317 Cherokee St.
St. Louis 63118
(314) 772-1439
Open: Monday through Saturday,
9:30 AM–5:30 PM

Abbey's Apron String is a large well-stocked kitchen shop on this street of antique shops. It has everything for cooking from butcher-block tables to canisters to cookbooks. There are pots, pans, baking utensils, accessories, gadgets, and more. From time to time on Saturdays, the shop hosts walk through cooking demonstrations.

Function Junction
Saint Louis Galleria
Richmond Heights 63117
(314) 863-6447
Open: Daily 10:00 AM–9:30 PM
(Sunday noon–6:00 PM)

Function Junction is a huge kitchen shop selling everything you could possibly need for equipping your kitchen, from small gadgets to butcher-block tables. Here you will find cooking utensils and equipment, small kitchen furniture, tableware, and bins and shelves for organizing your kitchen.

Kitchen Conservatory
8021 Clayton Rd.
Clayton 63117
(314) 862-2665
Open: Weekdays, 10:00 AM–6:00 PM
(Saturday 9:30 AM–5:30 PM and
Sunday noon–4:00 PM)

This pleasant shop has a nice selection of cookware and cookbooks. In addition, it serves as a local culinary center. The shop has a kitchen in the back that is used for cooking classes taught by very talented local chefs as well as nationally recognized guest chefs. There are even cooking classes and special food events for kids. From time to time, the Kitchen Conservatory sponsors bus trips to local culinary events. The shop puts out a newsletter about its classes and events. Call or stop in to get on the newsletter mailing list.

Peerless Restaurant Supplies
1124 South Grand
St. Louis 63104
(314) 664-0400
Open: Monday through Saturday,
8:00 AM–5:00 PM (9:00 AM–noon Saturday)

Peerless supplies kitchen equipment to restaurants, hotels, and institutions, but bargain hunters will love the bargain room, where close-outs and odds and ends are sold to the public at drastically reduced prices. Glasses, flatware, espresso cups, platters, plates, tea pots, ladles, pitchers, pizza pans, Chinese servers, and mugs are some of the items you might find in the bargain room. You might also find a used food slicer, cake decorating supplies, or an all purpose restaurant cleaner. You are also welcome to shop in the showroom for restaurant quality cookware and equipment.

Meat and Fish Markets

Bob's Seafood
*6655 Delmar (in the University City
Market in the Loop)
University City 63130
(314) 725-4844
Open: Daily, 9:30 AM–6:00 PM
(Wednesday through Saturday until 6:30 PM
and Sunday noon–5:00 PM)*

You can almost see the fish swimming—it's that fresh. That's why its worth the special trip to this small shop in the University City Market in the Loop for your fish purchase. The fish and seafood are air freighted every day, and if the weather is the least bit warm, your purchase will be packaged in ice to keep it at its maximum freshness. On a given day, you will have such fresh selections as salmon, flounder, clams, oysters, tuna, sea bass, scallops, crab, shrimp, rainbow trout, and lobster, and a freezer case that boasts such unusual selections as alligator, turtle, and frog legs. You can buy sauces, spices, mixes, and anything you might need as an accompaniment for your seafood.

Diamant's Kosher Meat Market and Delicatessen
*618 North and South Rd.
University City 63130
(314) 721-9624
Open: Sunday through Friday, 7:00 AM–5:00 PM
(Friday until 2:00 PM and Sunday until noon)*

This kosher butcher carries beef and poultry. It has a take-out counter for corned beef and other deli sandwiches. There is also a selection of kosher dry goods and frozen foods.

Lindy's Meat and Sausage
3401 Winnebago
St. Louis 63118
(314) 664-2172
Open: Thursday through Saturday,
9:00 AM–6:00 PM (Friday from 8:00 AM and
Saturday until 5:00 PM)

Some people go to work in the morning and do their job. Joseph Bittmann, the owner of Lindy's Meat and Sausage, goes to work in the morning and practices his art. From his humble neighborhood shop, this European-trained sausage maker is providing his neighborhood and other in-the-know St. Louisans with more than 100 varieties of homemade sausages that can be found in probably only a handful of shops in the country. He makes fresh sausages, smoked and air-dried sausages, and fully-cooked sausages.

The problem with shopping at Lindy's is that once you've tasted such sausages as his version of sasiza, a fresh Italian sausage that he stuffs with meat, spices, and Romano cheese, you'll no longer want to settle for anything else. Bittmann's Debriceni, a mildly smoked Hungarian sausage with spicy hot peppers in the deliciously seasoned mixture, is not to be missed. Beware of accepting a sample of landyaeger, a smoked ready-to-eat beef sausage that sits coiled innocently on top of the tall meat case. This terrific crunchy snack sausage is addictive. The franks at Lindy's are smooth and mildly flavored with the juicy snap that you only get in a hot dog in natural casing. The Hungarian bratwurst is flavored with sweet Hungarian paprika. He makes classic German sausages such as *blutwurst* (blood sausage), bockwurst, Thuringer, liverwurst, and more.

You will find ready-to-eat cooked sausages that have unusual casings such as ramerbraten that has meat and spices stuffed into a slab of smoked bacon. Fully cooked Canadian bacon and paprika bacon are ready to eat, as are a variety of headcheeses. Bittmann uses a natural hickory smoker to smoke his meats, and stacks of smoked ham shanks and cottage hams sit on the counter top enticing you to make a pot of bean soup. He also has smoked pork tenderloin, smoked pork chops, and will smoke special order specialty hams for you. The shop also has a full line of fresh meat and poultry, and a refrigerated case of food imported from Europe. This neighborhood St. Louis treasure is open only on Thursdays, Fridays, and Saturdays, and don't be surprised if you find yourself standing in a long Saturday morning line with half of St. Louis's European residents, who wait patiently because they know it's worth it.

Smoke House Market
16806 Chesterfield Airport Rd.
Chesterfield 63017
(314) 532-3314
Open: Tuesday through Sunday,
9:00 AM–6:00 PM (Sunday from 10:00 AM)

The powerful image of Thom and Jane Sehnert, the owners of the Smoke House and Annie Gunn's, as they were rescued by helicopter from the roof of their business, seems to epitomize the ravages of the great flood of 1993. The unique country store is back, supplying us with excellent fresh sausage, smoked bacons and hams, and other quality specialty foods. They make fresh sausages, some of which are smoked in a natural hickory smoker. The make delicious *chorizo*, a spicy Mexican-style sausage. Excellent mild beef wieners in natural casing are so juicy, they burst when broiled or grilled. The Smoke House's Cajun sausage and pepperoni are good, and the Italian sausage is a mild, sweet sausage. The bacon is smoked and cut thick, and cracked pepper gives it a nice bite. They sell excellent meat, including peppered steaks, free-range organic chicken, and smoked pork chops and ribs. The smoked trout is a special treat. A deli counter serves take-out sandwiches and soups, as well as sliced meats and cheeses. The shelves at this charming market are stocked with gourmet specialty foods, but it is the meat that makes the Smoke House worth a special trip. The market supplies the meat to

Annie Gunn's, the restaurant and bar next door. See the restaurants section in this book for more information.

Sol's Kosher Meat Market
8627 Olive St. Rd.
University City 63132
(314) 993-9977
Open: Sunday through Friday, 7:00 AM–5:00 PM
(Tuesday and Wednesday until 8:00 PM,
Friday until 2:30 PM and Sunday until 3:00 PM)

Sol's is a kosher butcher, deli, and caterer. You can buy fresh beef, lamb, veal, and poultry as well as some frozen foods and dry goods and then go to the deli for a corned beef sandwich or hot meal. The deli stays open late on Tuesday and Wednesday nights. You can cater a bar mitzvah, wedding, or bris, or just order your holiday kreplach from Sol's. Traditional Jewish foods such as kasha and bows, kishka, and knishes are available in large or small quantities.

Spring Prairie Farms (Lamb)
643 Hwy. AB
St. Clair 63077
(314) 629-2513

The sheep at Spring Prairie Farms are pasture raised and chemical free. You can order a whole or half lamb and have it custom packaged and delivered. It is usually processed and frozen, but you can make arrangements to have it delivered fresh. Call for information.

John Volpi and Company
5254 Daggett
St. Louis 63110
(314) 772-8550
Open: Tuesday through Saturday,
8:00 AM–4:30 PM (until 3:00 PM Saturday)

John Volpi and Company is one of those businesses that gives stature to the city and to the Hill, the neighborhood from which it has done business for 90 years. Volpi's makes wonderful Italian sausages, bacons, prosciuttos, and other cured meats. It is renowned for its classic prosciutto crudo, the unsmoked ham delicacy that is uncooked, but cured and ready to eat in transparently thin slices with melon or figs. For authentic pasta carbonara you will need pancetta, the unsmoked rolled bacon made at Volpi's. Another delicacy made here is bresaola, dried and aged beef filet that is served thinly sliced with Parmesan shavings and drizzled with olive oil.

At Volpi's they make salami to fit every taste; from the finely grained mildly spiced Genova to the coarser, spicier "farm-style" Siciliano. Mortadella, the large mild bologna, is another specialty. You can buy fresh sausages, including a mild salsiccia and a hot spicy Italian sausage. Volpi makes a hard-to-find Italian sausage of pork with white wine and spices called cotechino; this seasonal sausage needs two hours or more of boiling and is best served with beans or lentils. At the elegant shop, they sell their meats whole or by the slice. They also carry a selection of cheeses, pastas, chocolates, and gourmet specialty foods. Volpi sells by mail order. See the mail order section of this book for more information.

Note: See Produce Markets section in this book for meat and fish markets in Soulard Market

Coffee Shops and Coffee Houses

Ah—a good cup of coffee. Whether you have your favorite cup of the day in your bathrobe before you're articulate, or after a movie with dessert and perhaps a little music or poetry, there is good coffee to be had in St. Louis. There are coffee shops that sell a myriad of fresh roasted coffees to brew at home and coffee houses that offer a good cup of coffee, a bite to eat, and perhaps a bit of conversation. Here are a few of them.

Aesop's
6611 Clayton Rd.
Clayton 63117
(314) 727-0809
Open: Daily, 8:00 AM–midnight

Stop in for a cup of cappuccino (or other coffee specialty) and a morning scone, or have your coffee after a movie with dessert at this friendly coffeehouse. On Friday and Saturday evenings, there is usually music and on Sunday evening there is an "open mike." You can get a light meal here as well, and a table full of crayons and word games lets you know that kids are welcome.

Ibids
6687 Delmar Blvd.
University City 63130
(314) 862-2233
Open: Daily, 7:30 AM–midnight
(Sunday 11:00 AM–10:00 PM)

Ibids is attached to the wonderful Paul's Books, which provides the perfect ambiance for sipping a cup of espresso. You can also eat light fare, either at the counter or one of the 10 or so tables.

MoKaBe's Coffeehouse and Books
124 W. Jefferson, Suite 107
Kirkwood 63122
(314) 822-1895
Open: Daily, 10:00 AM–11:00 PM
(Friday and Saturday 9:00 AM–1:00 AM,
and 11:00 AM–9:00 PM Sunday)

Coffee and conversation are available in this smoky combination coffee house and bookshop. You can also have a snack. On Wednesday and Saturday nights there is live music and from time to time in the evening there is "open-mike" poetry and music.

Northwest Coffee Co.
8815 Ladue Rd.
Ladue 63124
(314) 725-8055
Open: Daily, 6:30 AM–7:30 PM
(Sunday 7:00 AM–6:00 PM)

You can buy coffee to brew in your favorite machine at home, and you can sit and enjoy a cup of coffee with a delicious scone, muffin, croissant, or cookie at one of the tables. The shop sells a dozen or so varietals and blends and will grind it for your type of coffeemaker or sell you the beans for you to grind yourself. You can also buy coffee makers and accessories here.

Shenandoah Coffee Company
2300 South Grand
St. Louis 63104
(314) 664-3223
Open: Monday through Saturday,
7:00 AM–6:00 PM (Saturday 9:00 AM–5:00 PM)

This friendly neighborhood coffee and tea shop has 30 or so varietals, blends, and flavored coffees and another 30 types of bulk tea. The shop has a good selection of coffeepots, teapots, and accessories. They serve coffee, tea, and a bite to eat at a few tables in the shop. Various coffees are available for sampling.

Spilling the Beans
395 Euclid Ave.
St. Louis 63108
(314) 367-2828
Open: Daily, 8:30 AM–9:00 PM
(Saturday and Sunday from 9:30 AM)

Spilling the Beans has a large selection of coffee—more than 40 varieties and blends. The flavored coffees at this shop are flavored with natural ingredients rather than syrups. The shop carries a variety of bulk tea, as well as coffeepots, teapots, and accessories. There are a few tables where you can relax with a scone, muffin, or slice of cheesecake and a cup of coffee.

Note: Freshly roasted coffee is also available at the Cheese Place, the Roasting House, and Starr's. See the Specialty Foods section of this book for more information.

Fresh from the Country

Produce Markets

Kirkwood Farmers' Market

111 S. Geyer
Kirkwood 63122
(314) 822-5855
Open: April through October, Thursday,
Friday, and Saturday, 8:00 AM–6:00 PM,
Saturday until 5:00 PM

Beginning in April, you can buy fresh produce from the green grocers at the market, and as local produce begins to ripen, the farmers bring in more and more of their fresh produce to sell. Some of them set up their own stands, and others sell to the greengrocers, who sell to you.

Soulard Market

730 Carroll Street
St. Louis 63104
(314) 622-4180
Open: Tuesday through Saturday,
8:00 AM–5:30 PM, (Saturday 6:00 AM–6:00 PM)

Soulard Market is the jewel in the crown of midwestern farmers markets. It is a St. Louis treasure, one that is intertwined with the city's history. Over the years it has had its ups and downs, but the two-block-long market with its 148 individual stands where, all year round, you can buy fresh fruits and vegetables, spices, cheeses, eggs, poultry, meat, fish, and flowers, has persevered. Although there is some question about whether Soulard is more than 200 years old or merely 150 years old, one thing is clear: Soulard is the historic crossroads where the ageold ritual of consumer meeting farmer and merchant takes place.

At Soulard your senses will be awakened by the perfume of fresh spices, the color of fresh produce, and the sounds of merchants selling their wares. One of the pleasures of Soulard is that you don't know what the farmers will bring to market each day. Yes, the essentials will be there. But it is a place to surprise and delight a friend with a basket of fresh sunflowers or a bouquet of herbs. It is a place where a man waiting for his wife will be asked by half a dozen strangers where he bought his bag of fresh locally grown pecans. It is where inventive cooks go with an open mind to buy the freshest local harvest picked that very morning. And, just when you are beginning to think that the "season" for marketing is finished, you will begin to see holiday products invade the stalls and the excitement of the holiday season will take you back to another century.

Produce at Soulard comes from two sources: the farmers who are there from the first of spring's earliest harvest through the holidays (or until their crops are sold), and the green grocers who are there year round. The **Scharf** family from Millstadt, Illinois, will start the season at Soulard in April with fresh asparagus, and then follow in May with sweet, juicy strawberries, and continue through Thanksgiving with a variety of fresh produce. Among the green grocers there are those who carry top quality produce, like the **Vitales** who have been at Soulard for three generations, and others who carry produce of varying quality and price. Whether you are seeking bargains, fresh locally grown produce, organic produce, or all three, you'll find what you need at Soulard.

The **Kruse** family operates one of the most interesting produce stands at Soulard. Known as the "organic gardener," Arlene Kruse wears a miner's flashlight on her forehead to pick produce in the dark before heading to market from her Illinois farm. Bountiful bunches of fresh herbs, terrific tat-soi lettuce, mizzuna lettuce, escarole, and arugula, tender turnips, purple and white eggplant, sweet and hot peppers, leeks, bouquets of fresh zinnias or cox comb, tiny tomatoes, and a host of other organically grown vegetables, herbs, and flowers make up the Kruses' bounty.

The **Kruger** family also sells organic produce such as sweet and hot peppers, Chinese okra, and Asian eggplants. You might also find sassafras root and hickory or cherry wood for smoking or barbecuing at their stand. At the stand of **Stone Ledge Farm**, another organic farm, you will find fruit such as red raspberries, strawberries, and concord grapes. Look for shiitake mushrooms, greens, squash, herbs, red okra, snow peas, and other seasonal produce. At the modest stand of **Aunt May's Produce** you can find fresh chestnuts, hickory nuts, and black walnuts. She sells fresh chicken eggs and, from time to time, has duck and goose eggs. The **Sieberts** have a number of stands at the market from which you can buy fresh free-range chickens, turkeys, quails, ducks, Cornish hens, and capons. The Sieberts do their own hickory smoking and produce delicious smoked turkey, as well as other smoked meats. They have fresh eggs and shelled fresh lima beans, butter beans, and black-eyed peas. At the stand of **Wall-Vern Farms** you can buy live or "fresh-dressed" free-range chickens, turkeys, ducks, and geese. They also sell fresh horseradish root and ground horseradish; local peach blossom, apple blossom, and buckwheat honey; fresh butter; locally-grown stoneground corn meal; and sorghum. You can find black walnuts from the farm of the **Ziegler** family as well as Missouri pecans, sweet potatoes, eggs, and close to the holidays, the Zieglers have "fresh trapped coon" and other seasonal products. During the holiday season, the **Frandeka Fish Market** sports a sign that reads "order now, Lutefisk and finan haddie." The shop has a large selection of fish to fit all tastes and budgets and includes alligator, turtle, frog legs, and shark.

Look for fresh seasonal strawberries, raspberries, blackberries, blueberries, and gooseberries at various stands, or indulge yourself with a bushel of famous Calhoun County peaches. Fruit that is locally grown can be picked at peak ripeness, so consider preserving its perfect flavor in a jar of jam. If you don't know how to make jam, you might be able to learn at one of the summer classes taught at Soulard. Watch for notices of various classes in local newspapers or call the office in the summer for more information.

In the center of Soulard are a number of shops. Let the captivating fragrance from the **Soulard Spice Shop** lead you into the store that offers a large selection of fresh and reasonably priced spices, many of them sold in bulk. The shop has a nice selection of cheeses and imported pastas, as well as gourmet items. Snack on a soft pretzel or a soft pretzel stuffed with sausitza from Gus' Pretzel Shop that is sold at the **Schmitz Soulard Sip and Snack Stand** and watch the world go by while resting on one of the available benches. The **Frandeka** shop in the center of Soulard is the place to buy goat, chittlins, cracklings, as well as smoked jowl and salt jowl. The lines are long on Saturday mornings at **M. Schmitz's Market**, where you can buy farm fresh chicken, home smoked sausages, and a large variety of fresh meats, including (if you are inclined) the whole tail of an ox! Soulard Market is a timeless treasure, a constantly changing spectacle, and quite simply, a fun place to shop.

University City Produce Market
6655 Delmar
Open: Thursday, Friday, and Saturday,
8:00 AM–5:30 PM (or so)

Behind the enclosed University City Market in the Loop are fresh produce stands. In the summer they are bustling with activity as local farmers bring their produce to market. And even in winter, there is always at least one green grocer who sells fresh produce behind a makeshift canvas wall. The produce is considerably less expensive than it is in grocery stores.

Note: The following market is not a produce market. It is a full service grocery store, with an excellent selection of produce.

Garden Market
8823 Ladue Rd.
Ladue 63124
(314) 721-7887
Open: Daily, 7:00 AM–10:00 PM

The Garden Market is a full service grocery store, but in the dead of winter when you need specific fresh herbs or produce or if you just can't get to a farmers market, this is the place to find a good selection of fresh herbs and produce. Here you also can buy such unusual produce as white asparagus, portobello mushrooms, yellow tomatoes, cactus, arugula, Jerusalem artichokes, shallots, and much more. During their respective seasons you might find 10 varieties of fresh chilis, six colors of bell peppers, numerous varieties of mushrooms and baby vegetables, and a dozen types of apples and pears. There is usually a good selection of fresh lettuces, and for those who don't mind the added expense, there is a bin to buy ready-mixed fresh field greens. If the season isn't right for finding the exact item you need, the Garden Market will surely have a worthy substitute.

Missouri Farms

Centennial Farms
199 Jackson St.
Augusta 63332
(314) 228-4338
Open: Mid-April through June, weekends only, Saturday,
10:00 AM–5:00 PM and Sunday, 1:00 PM–5:00 PM (except,
during strawberry season, open daily, 8:00 AM–5:00 PM)
July through October, daily, 10:00 AM–5:00 PM

Although Centennial Farms is more than 130 years old, it is not stuck in the past. It owners are continually adding new crops, providing us with the opportunity to expand our culinary experience. The list of interesting and hard-to-find produce grown at Centennial Farms includes white asparagus, 100 varieties of herbs, 12 varieties of sweet and hot peppers, basketball-sized watermelons including the wonderful sugar baby, and a few unusual varieties of apples. The season begins in mid-April with asparagus, which lasts six to eight weeks. They grow both green and white asparagus. If you time it right, you can buy fresh asparagus when you go to pick strawberries which are usually ready in mid-May and available for three to four weeks. In mid-June look for U-pick sour cherries. Black and red raspberries are available already picked, usually from mid-June through July. They also have fall red raspberries which last until frost. Peaches come in mid-July, Concord grapes in mid-August, and apples begin in August. The varieties of apples they grow at Centennial Farms are Jonathan, Red Delicious, Golden Delicious, Lodi, Gala, Ozark Gold, Lurared, Empire, Winesap, Arkansas Black, Rome, and Blushing Golden. They also have York Imperial and Fuji trees, which are still too young to produce crops.

Throughout the season you will find other fresh produce including tomatoes, okra, beans, broccoli, sweet corn, eggplant, turnips, and more. They have herb festivals for three weekends beginning the last weekend in April, when they hold workshops and sell herb plants. In October they have a Pumpkin Fantasy Land with pumpkins painted like nursery rhyme characters, and hayrides to the pumpkin patch where kids can choose their own pumpkins. They make their own cider, apple butter, and fruit and berry preserves. Call for information on availability of berries. To get there take I-40 to Hwy. 94. Go left, drive 18 miles to Augusta and watch for signs to the farm.

Engelhart Farms
2940 W. Osage
Pacific 63069
(314) 742-4047
Open: July 1 through October, daily, 9:00 AM–dusk,
and special order asparagus in mid-April until June

They raise standard as well as unusual varieties of vegetables at Engelhart Farms. The variety of tomatoes is staggering—with 40 varieties you can find them small round and small pearshaped in red, yellow, and pink; canning varieties; beefsteak varieties in red and yellow; and low-acid varieties. They grow sweet peppers in red, yellow, white, "chocolate," and purple, and hot Hungarian wax and jalapeño. Eggplant comes in typical bell, white, pink, European, and Asian. They grow six varieties of summer squash, 12 varieties of winter squash, green beans, sweet corn, spineless okra, and other vegetables. They also grow cantaloupe and watermelons including the basketball-sized sugar baby watermelon. The market stand does not open until July 1, but you can special-order asparagus beginning sometime in mid-April for about six weeks. To get there take I-44 to the Pacific exit. Go until the first stop light and then turn right to Hwy. 66. Drive for two miles until you see the sign.

Fresh Mushroom Farm
(314) 464-0272
Phone orders only

This unusual farm specializes in exotic mushrooms, fresh herbs, edible flowers, and other specialty items that can be ordered for delivery to St. Louis and the surrounding areas. They cultivate shiitake mushrooms and also have oyster, portobello, crimini, and enoki year round. They have seasonal wild mushrooms. In spring look for morels, porcini (cepes), giant puffballs, and coral mushrooms. In early fall, you can buy chanterelles, chicken of the woods, hen of the woods, as well as coral, lobster, and porcini mushrooms. In late fall, they have cauliflower, chanterelle, coral, hedgehog, matsutake, and porcini mushrooms, as well as white truffles. Available in the winter are black trumpet, chanterelle, hedgehog, and matsutake mushrooms, as well as black and white truffles. Throughout the year they have fresh frozen black and white truffles, and porcini and matsutake mushrooms. Dried mushrooms come whole, in pieces, or as powder. They also have dried chilis, Arborio, basmati, purple sticky, and wild rice. Beans, lentils, dried fruits and berries, dried tomatoes, and corn products are available. They sell two dozen varieties of fresh herbs all year round. For more information, call for a product list.

George's Orchard
P. O. Box 266
Gray Summit 63039
(314) 742-4358
Open: Labor Day through Christmas,
Monday through Saturday, 8:30 AM–5:00 PM

They grow about 20 varieties of apples at this fourth-generation family farm. They have Lodi, Mantet, Jerseymac, Summer Treat, Royal Gala, Jonathan, Golden Delicious, Blushing Golden, Empire, Red Delicious, Lurared, Stamen Winesap, Winesap, York Imperial, Arkansas Black, Granny Smith, Mutsu,

Braeburn, Fuji, Rome Beauty, and according to orchard owner Jim Daniels, "a few good-tasting mystery varieties." They make their own apple butter and cider. To get there take I-44 to the Pacific exit and go until the first stop light. Turn right to Hwy. 66, and drive for three miles until you see the sign. They also grow asparagus, which is available by special order usually in mid-April for a few week. For asparagus special orders, call 742-2240.

Mueller's Organic Farm
233 S. Dade Ave.
Ferguson 63135
(314) 522-9538
Open: April through October, daily,
noon until dusk, (Sunday from 10:00 AM)

This organic farm begins its season in April with asparagus and vegetable and herb bedding plants. Rhurbarb and strawberries are next. Throughout the season at the roadside stand, you can buy such produce as herbs, corn, green beans, carrots, beets, kale, collards, okra, tomatoes, a variety of sweet and hot peppers, broccoli, turnips, potatoes, squash, and more. They have blackberries, gooseberries, black and red raspberries, red plums, Kiefer pears, and black walnuts. To get there, take I-70 to Florrisant Blvd. and go north until Suburban Rd., then turn left. Turn right at Dade and turn left to the farm.

Pickle Barrel Produce
445 Old State Rd.
Ellisville 63021
(314) 227-2448
Open: June through October,
daily, noon until dusk

The produce is organically grown at this farm, which usually opens in early June. Look for green beans, tomatoes, white sweet corn, Brussels sprouts, lima beans, okra, sweet and hot peppers, cantaloupe, eggplant, squash, and more. There are a few peaches, plums, and apples, as well as fresh horseradish root. At Pickle Barrel Produce, you can buy the pastel-colored fresh eggs of Araucana chickens from South America. These chickens, known as the "Easter-egg fowl," lay blue, green, pink, olive, or gold eggs. To get there, take Manchester Rd. west past Clarkson Rd. to Old State, go left, and drive until you see the farm.

Prouhet Vegetable Farm
13038 Taussig Rd.
Bridgeton 63044
(314) 739-4978
Open: Mid-June (or July) until Thanksgiving, daily,
10:00 AM–7:00 PM (Sunday until 2:00 PM) and closed
Sundays after Halloween

They have a large selection of fresh produce at this farm, and you can pick your own green beans, lima beans, okra, crowder peas, greens, turnips, mustard greens, kale, and more. Most of these vegetables are also available already picked. They have sweet corn, eggplant, a variety of hot peppers and sweet peppers, tomatoes, beets, broccoli, cauliflower, sweet potatoes, and various types of squash. You can buy blackberries, cantaloupe, seedless watermelons, and a basketball-sized watermelon called a "sugar baby" with a thin rind and tender, sweet flesh. In October they have pumpkins already picked or you can take your kids to the pumpkin patch to pick their own. They also have a hayride and straw castle for kids. To get there take I-70 to St. Charles Rock Rd. Go north to Taussig Rd. and then turn right. When you get to Ferguson Ln. go left until you get to Prouhet Farm Rd. (formerly Taussig) and watch for signs.

Sommers Brothers
4470 Blase Station Rd.
St. Charles 63301
(314) 250-3206
Open: April through mid-June, daily, 7:00 AM–7:00 PM

They're never surprised to hear a shout from their strawberry fields: it's just another unwary strawberry picker coming across a toad. The strawberries at Sommers Farm are insecticide free, because when they built a pond on the farm years ago, toads came and then decided they liked the bugs that grew on the strawberry plants. U-pick strawberries are ready around mid-May and last for about three weeks. They grow five varieties of strawberries and actually expect you to try them so you'll be able to tell which you like best. You can also buy herb and vegetable bedding plants, beginning in April. Some of the herb plants they sell are four varieties of basil, two varieties of oregano, six mints, two tarragons, two oreganos, a few parsleys, a few sages, garlic chives, onion chives, bay laurel, chervil, dill, coriander, camomile, lavender, and a variety of scented geraniums. To get there, take I-270 to 370, and get off at Hwy. 94 north. Drive 4½ miles and go left on Blase Station Rd., and look for the green-houses on the right.

Stuckmeyer's Farm Market
249 Schneider Dr.
Fenton 63026
(314) 349-1225
Open: April through October, daily,
9:00 AM–6:00 PM (Sunday, 10:00 AM–4:00 PM)

This farm market opens in April to sell bedding plants. They have U-pick strawberries around mid-May. Fresh produce throughout the growing season includes rhubarb, green beans, spinach, beets, eggplant, okra, hot and sweet peppers, tomatoes, turnips, cantaloupe, watermelon, potatoes, and more. In October they have weekend hayrides at a U-pick pumpkin patch. To get there, take I-270 to Hwy. 21. At Hwy. 141 go west to Schneider Dr. and turn left until you see the farm. Call for U-pick strawberry information.

Thies Farm and Greenhouses
4215 N. Hanley Rd.
unincorporated Normandy 63121
(314) 428-9878
Open: March 1 through Christmas eve,
daily, 9:00 AM–6:00 PM (Sunday, 10:00 AM–4:00 PM)

Even though the city has grown around this 120-year-old farm near Lambert Airport, it continues to provide people in the know with fresh farm produce and U-pick berries. The season begins in March when the shop opens to sell bedding plants of herbs, vegetables, perennials, and annuals. Asparagus starts around mid-April and U-pick strawberries are usually ready to be picked beginning in mid-May. Black raspberries are next, followed by blackberries and black raspberries. They are sold ready-picked, usually beginning in mid-to-late June. You can pick your own fall red raspberries from about August 1 through the first frost. Peaches, nectarines, and a few apricots are also grown on the farm, and they ripen sometime around late July.

Throughout the summer and fall, the shop is filled with a complete selection of fresh produce grown on this farm, their other farm in Creve Coeur, or other local farms. Look for sweet corn, a dozen varieties of sweet and hot peppers, fresh herbs, green beans, broccoli, tomatoes, eggplant, okra, sweet potatoes, and specialty food items. In the fall, Thies Farm has a pumpkinland complete with straw mazes, wagon rides, and other activities for kids.

Wind Ridge Farm
P.O. Box 186
New Melle 63365
(314) 828-5753
Open: Around mid-July for three weeks,
call for availability

Pick your own peaches beginning in mid-July. The farm is located near the August Busch Wildlife area and Daniel Boone's home, so if you time it right, you can enjoy summer's peach bounty when enjoying a day in the country. To get there, take I-40 west to Hwy. 94 south. Go to Hwy. D and turn right. Drive 10 miles to New Melle and take Hwy. F left and watch for signs.

Illinois Farms

Bohn's Farm
1656 Pleasant Ridge Rd.
Marysville 62234
(618) 344-2572
Open: April through June, daily,
8:00 AM–7:00 PM

They open in April to sell hundreds of varieties of bedding plants, including vegetables, perennials, and annuals. But you can time your plant shopping with asparagus or strawberry season for a special treat. The ready-picked asparagus are usually ready beginning in mid-April and last until June. Strawberries are usually available May 20 for four weeks. You can pick them yourself or buy them ready-picked. Call ahead for availability information. To get there take I-55 (70) to Rt. 159 and go north to Maryville. Then go left on West Main St. and look for signs.

Braeutigam Orchards
2765 Turkey Hill Lane
Belleville 62221
(618) 233-4059
Open: Mid-June through October 31,
daily, 8:00 AM–7:00 PM (Sunday until 6:00 PM),
after October 31, call for apples until Christmas

The season begins with U-pick blackberries and cherries at this family orchard. U-pick peaches and raspberries are next, followed by ready-picked nectarines. They also sell vegetables such as eggplants, tomatoes, peppers, sweet corns, green beans, and pumpkins. In the fall look for plums, Concord grapes, and a dozen or so apple varieties including Gala, Empire, Golden Delicious, Red Delicious, Jonathan, Granny Smith, Winesap,

Jerseymac, Jonagrimes, Prima, and Ozark Gold. The orchard is three miles southeast of Belleville on Rt. 15.

Eckerts Orchards
3101 Greenmount Rd.
Belleville 62220
(618) 234-4406 (U-pick information line),
(618) 233-0513 (country store office)
Open: Year round, daily (closed Sunday, January
through March), 9:00 AM–5:00 PM (hours extended
in spring and summer)

With 50,000 trees (spread on five farms), Eckerts is one of the largest U-pick apple and peach orchards in the country. They also grow strawberries, blackberries, and pumpkins, that you can pick yourself or buy ready-picked. They grow 11 varieties of apples, but only the standards, such as Red Delicious, Golden Delicous, and Jonathan, are available U-pick. Ask for Granny Smith, Fuji, Mutsu, and Empire, if you are interested in buying these interesting varieties ready-picked. You can buy green and white asparagus, ears of sweet corn, green beans, cantaloupes, watermelons, nectarines, and specialty food items at the country store.

The country store is open year round, but the U-pick fresh produce begins with strawberries at the end of May. Blackberries begin at the end of June, peaches begin in mid-July, apples begin in September, and pumpkins in October. There are festivals and harvest events throughout the summer and fall at the farm. Call for U-pick information and a brochure about the events. The orchard is located three miles southeast of Belleville on Hwy. 15.

Emerald Valley Pecans
At the east side of the Kampsville Ferry
(217) 983-2831 or 945-6397
Open: Call in late October and November
for availability

The great flood of 1993 almost claimed this grove—the largest pecan grove this far north in America. Some trees drowned in 14 feet of water, but others lived. And though it might take a few years to regain a large pecan crop, this local treasure is sure to provide local residents and others in the know with fresh Illinois pecans once again.

When "R.B." (Richard Best) came as a farmhand to this piece of land beside the river in the early 1920s, he loved the native pecan trees that he found. Years later, after he became a successful corn hybridizer who had accumulated 3,000 acres of rich farmland, he set aside 300 acres for pecan trees. Grafting was his hobby and local residents can still recall the vision of 350-pound R.B. perched on his ladder grafting his beloved pecan trees. His grove eventually contained 36 varieties of pecans. Beginning in October or November, after a hard frost or two, the pecans start falling and are ready for "picking." You can buy them ready-picked at the blazing white shed with green trim that is on the north side of Rt. 108 at the Kampsville Ferry, or you can pick them yourself and keep one-third and give back two-thirds. Call to find out if there are pecans.

Fletcher's Family Farm
R.R. 2, Box 735
Marysville 62234
(618) 344-3797
Open: Early-July through September,
daily, dawn until dusk

Pick your own thornless blackberries and red raspberries at this small family farm. The Fletchers don't use pesticides in growing their berries. Blackberries usually begin in early July and are available until mid-August when the red raspberries begin. They are usually available until the end of September. Call for availability. To get there take I-55 (70) to Rt. 159 and go north to Maryville. Go left on West Main St. and look for signs.

Fournie Farms
R.R. 3, Box 120
Collinsville 62234
(618) 344-8527
Open: June through Halloween, daily,
9:00 AM–7:00 PM

Collinsville, Illinois's claim to culinary fame is that it's the horseradish capital of the world. Although they grow it, most of it is sold to processors who grind and bottle the pungent, spicy root. But if you want to grind your own in your food processor, you can buy fresh horseradish root at Fournie Farms. You can also buy a bevy of other fresh produce such as tomatoes, sweet corn, okra, green beans, broccoli, lettuce, cauliflower, potato, sweet potato, cantaloupe, watermelon, honeydew, and pumpkin at the roadside stand. Take I-55 to the Horseshoe Lake Rd. exit, and make a left at the stop sign. Go two roads until you see the stand.

Krueger's Orchard
2914 Airport Rd.
Godfrey 62035
(618) 466-3576
Open: End of June through December 31
(and after by appointment if apples are available),
daily, 9:00 AM–dark (Sunday from 10:00 AM)

Although this thousand-tree orchard doesn't open full-time until the end of June, you can call and order Montmorency sour cherries, which are sometimes ready earlier. They also grow peaches, apples, and pears. Peachs are usually available from the end of July until the first of September. The apple varieties are

Earliblaze, Jonathan, Red Delicious, Golden Delicious, Arkansas Black, and Blushing Golden. They grow their own produce such as sweet corn, tomatoes, green beans, cantaloupe, watermelon, cucumbers, and pumpkins, and sell them from an open market attached to their house. They make fresh apple cider as long as they have apples. To get there, take Rt. 67 north to Godfrey and watch for the signs.

Madison Farms
3402 Ridgeview Rd.
Edwardsville 62025
(618) 656-1323
Open: By arrangement

Becky and Dave Duckworth specialize in growing fresh herbs and rare vegetables. You can buy either the plants to grow in your own garden or fresh-picked herbs and vegetables. They will also locate seeds for and contract-grow hard-to-find specialty herbs and vegetables. They have an excellent selection of 80 culinary herbs that includes 15 basil varieties, 10 thymes, arugula, chervil, cumin, French tarragon, mustard, nine types of mint, four sages, watercress, and much more. They grow edible flowers such as nasturtiums. They grow 20 varieties of tomatoes including some that are yellow, white, purple, pink, and multi-colored. Their selection of sweet and hot peppers is very extensive and includes sweet bell peppers in yellow, orange, red, white, purple, and brown, and hot peppers in 16 or so varieties. If you visit the Duckworth farm during iris season (usually May and June), you will be treated to the spectacular sight of the Duckworths' prize-winning iris collection. Call for an appointment and for directions.

McAdams Orchard
R.R. 2, Box 208
Seminary Rd.
Brighton 62012
Open: Mid-May through November,
daily, 9:00 AM–6:00 PM (Sunday from noon),
dawn until dusk for berry picking

McAdams Orchard has the largest and best selection of apple varieties in the area. Located just seven miles from Alton, this wonderful orchard has close to 50 varieties of apples as well as a spectacular variety of other fruits including red, yellow, purple, and black raspberries; 15 varieties of peaches; nectarines; apricots; plums; red and yellow sweet cherries; sour cherries; eight varieties of pears; and hard-to-find berries such as gooseberries, elderberries, and blackberries. In addition to fruit, the orchard grows asparagus, tomatoes, hot peppers, hot-hot peppers, sweet peppers, squashes, pumpkins, and gourds (for making bird houses).

The season begins around mid-May when asparagus is for sale ready-picked. The berries begin around mid-June and are everbearing, so they are available into September. Berries are sold U-pick, but some can be special ordered. Apples are both U-pick and ready-picked. Although some of the varieties grown at this orchard are fairly common, others are very rare and very hard to find locally. Some of the varieties are Loriglo, Akane, Paula Red, Gala, Mollie's Delicious, Red Delicious, Golden Delicious, Empire, Blushing Golden, Jonagold, Firmgold, Jonalicious, Ozark Gold, Grimes Golden, Newtown Pippin, Mutsu, Spigold, Northern Spy, Fuji, York Imperial, Granny Smith, Arkansas Black, Winesap, Winter Banana, Gourmet Golden, and Criterion. (See Apple Varieties section at the end of this book for descriptions of apples.)

The McAdamses have a barn store from which they sell fresh produce and their own apple cider. Call for the availability of berries and particular varieties of apples. To get there take Rt.

67 to Brighton and go to Brown Rd. Go one mile east on Brown Road and then south on Seminary until you see the orchard.

Mestel-Murphy Orchard
522 S. Mulberry Rd.
Collinsville 62234
(618) 344-0657
Open: End of May through mid-November,
daily, 9:00 AM–7:00 PM

This 500-tree family orchard begins the season with rhubarb at the end of May. In mid-July peaches ripen and are available until the end of August. They grow a dozen varieties of apples, two varieties of pears, and four varieties of plums. Mrs. Murphy keeps trying to grow nectarines, despite their finicky nature, so be sure to ask if the trees produced a crop when you visit because ripe-from-the-tree nectarines are wonderful. The apple varieties include Jonathan, Golden Delicious, Red Delicious, Rome, Stamen, Winesap, Lodi, Earliblaze, and Granny Smith, as well as Gala, Fuji, and Braeburn, which are young and will take a few years to produce. A yellow plum variety begins in July; a dark red variety begins in August, and two varieties of prune plums are available at the end of August. Pears begin at the end of August. The Murphys make their own cider. To get there, take I-55 to Collinsville and out East Main. Turn left at Lebanon until you see the General Store at South Mulberry where you turn right and go for two miles until you see the sign.

Mills Apple Farm
11477 Pocahontas Rd.
Marine 62061
(314) 887-4732
Open: July through December 24,
daily, 9:00 AM–5:30 PM

Mills Apple Farm has 17 varieties of apples and 10 varieties of peaches. They also bake their own delicious pies and apple breads, which they sell from a bakery attached to a shed, where you can buy apples and cider. The apple pies are excellent—they are heavy with fresh fruit, and not overly sweet—and the apple-nut bread is moist, spicy, and delicious. At Mills Apple Farm you can buy apples ready-picked or you can pick them yourself. The varieties are Earliblaze, Ginger Gold, Jonathan, Lustre Estar, Ozark Gold, Gala, Jonared, Empire, Spartan, Jonagold, Red Delicious, Golden Delicious, Fuji, Granny Smith, Braeburn, Blushing Golden, and Winesap. The farm also has a small petting farm, hayrides on some fall weekends, and a water maze for kids. Call ahead for U-pick information and for availability of particular varieties. To get there take I-270 to Hwy. 4 (exit 21) and go left. At Hwy. 143 go right to downtown Marine. At the four-way stop sign go left and follow the signs.

Pence Orchards
I-55 and Spangle Rd.
Livingston 62058
(618) 637-2686
Open: Mid-May until June and mid-July
through November, daily,
7:00 AM–7:00 PM (during strawberry season)
and 10:00 AM–6:00 PM for all else

The season begins in mid-May with strawberries, which you can pick yourself or buy ready-picked. Red raspberries usually begin in late June and last until October. They are U-pick or ready-picked. They have sweet corn in July. The Pences grow the following varieties of apples: Gala, Red Delicious, Golden Delicious, Jonathan, Fuji, and Granny Smith. Apples are U-pick or ready-picked. In October, you can pick your own pumpkin from the field or buy it at the produce stand. To get there take I-55 to exit 37 and then go one-half mile north on West Frontage Road.

Red Barn
9508 Triad Lane
St. Jacob 62281
(618) 644-2982
Open: Mid-April through October 31,
daily, 8:00 AM–7:00 PM

The Strackeljahn family is the largest asparagus grower in the area. Look for asparagus in mid-April. It usually is available until strawberry season begins at about the end of May. Strawberries are available U-pick or ready-picked. Purple raspberries, which are a cross between black and red raspberries, begin in July and red raspberries begin in August. Throughout the summer and fall, you will find fresh produce such as sweet corn, cantaloupes, tomatoes, green peppers, green beans, sweet potatoes, and squashes at the Red Barn.

Creepy pumpkin lovers will like the pumpkin variety developed and grown on the Strackeljahn farm with lots of " warts." Or, if you'd like to develop a few warts of your own, try the horseradish grown on the farm. Horseradish root is harvested in the fall and winter, so if you'd like the root, call to order it, or if you'd like it processed in jars, you can buy it at the Red Barn. To get there, take I-55 (70) to Rt. 40 and go straight six miles until you see a red barn across from Triad High School.

Scharf's Farm
8128 State Rt. 163
Millstadt 62260
(618) 538-5698
Open: Early April until Thanksgiving,
daily, 8:00 AM–6:00 PM

The asparagus arrives early at Scharf's—usually around the beginning of April. It is sold ready-picked and is available until the middle of June. You can usually pick your own strawberries beginning in mid-May. They last about three weeks. U-pick thornless blackberries are due around June 20th and last for two months. You can buy berries ready picked as well. Peaches are available in July, August, and September and you can buy sweet corn, cantaloupe, watermelon, sweet potato, pumpkin, and other seasonal vegetables at the farm. The Scharfs sell their produce at Soulard. Call for availability of berries. To get to the farm take I-255 to Rt. 157 and go south. Go to Rt. 163 (towards Millstadt). The farm is four miles north of Millstadt on Rt. 163.

Schlueter's Orchard
601 Obstweg off Schlueter Germain Rd.
Belleville 62220
(618) 277-4864
Open: Mid-June through October (when fruit is in),
daily, 8:00 AM–8:00 PM (fall until dusk). Call for
availability of berries.

The blueberries are ready for blueberry pie on the Fourth of July. In fact, they are usually ready for you to pick in mid-June and are available for one month. Thornless blackberries are available for U-pick in late July and last about three to four weeks. U-pick peaches are ripe around mid-July through late August. The Schlueters also grow apples. They have Red Delicious, Golden Delicious, Jonagold, Empire, Ozark Gold, and Lurared. Call for berry and apple variety availability information. To get there take I-255 to Hwy. 15. Then take Hwy. 159 south for two miles and look for signs.

Weigel Orchards
R.R. 1, Box 72
Golden Eagle 62036
(618) 883-2347
Open: Mid-July through Labor Day,
daily, 8:00 AM–6:00 PM (call for crop information)

Nectarines are hard to grow in this area, but luckily for us, a few stubborn orchardists keep trying. If you've never tasted a nectarine ripe from the tree, you don't know what you're missing. In mid-July, you can get them at Weigel Orchard. They have them for about a month. You also can buy peaches from about mid-July until about September 20. They grow four varieties of plums—summer and fall varieties. To get to the orchard, take Hwy. 367 to Alton. Then take the river road to Grafton, take the Brussels Ferry and go four miles on the blacktop. Turn left on Auher Rd. and look for signs.

Shopping for Morels

From the banks of the Illinois River and the small islands in the river, local mushroom hunters bring in hundreds of pounds of morel mushrooms during mushroom season, usually from the second week in April through Mothers' Day. Local lore tells of 10-inch mushrooms found in the area. The mushroom hunters, many of whom make their living off the river, sell their mushrooms through local taverns. The mushrooms cost from $8 to $15 per pound, depending on the year's crop. The arrangements are informal, but if you're interested in taking a drive to pick up morels, call any of the taverns listed below. If they don't have any for sale, ask them who might.

Apple Blossom Tavern and Restaurant
Hardin, IL
(618) 576-9098

Brussels Tavern
Brussels, IL
(618) 883-2233

Fin Inn
Grafton, IL
(618) 786-2030

Korner Tavern
Hardin, IL
(618) 576-9005

Louie's Kampsville Inn
Kampsville, IL
(618) 653-4413
When at Louie's stop in for fried catfish or buffalo fish, a heaping platter of fried onion rings, and a slice of apple pie.

The Palace
Hamburg, IL
(618) 232-1122

Apple Varieties

Locally grown apples provide us with a wonderful opportunity to taste apples at their best—fresh off the tree. The variety of tastes and textures that apples provide is a wonderful surprise to people who have grown up eating Red Delicious as the standard. In the St. Louis area, we are lucky to have a number of growers who are branching out and trying new apple varieties. You can find approximately 60 varieties within a 50-mile radius of St. Louis. Although some apples need to be eaten within weeks of picking for the best flavor, others improve with age or can be stored for months with no loss of flavor. This list will help you identify good "keepers." The types of apples grown at each orchard are listed, but it is best to call ahead to find out which varieties are available. So take a drive to an apple orchard in the fall and stock up on as many apples as your refrigerator will hold. In January, when grocery store apples are mushy and expensive, you'll be glad you did!

Akane-This small apple is a slightly tart Jonathan cross that is available in mid-August.

Arkansas Black-As unusual in flavor as it is beautiful in appearance, this apple is such a dark red that it appears purple. It is too hard to eat when harvested, but after a few months in storage, the flesh is dense, not especially juicy, and has a slight almond flavor.

Ashmead's Kernel-This rather ugly golden-brown russet apple, according to Tom Vorbeck (of Applesource) is "not for sissy palates." It is a juicy, sugary apple that has been grown for more than 200 years.

Blushing Golden-This is a popular, pretty yellow apple with a pink blush. It is similar to Golden Delicious but has more snap, is tarter, and is a better keeper.

Bounty-This good, crisp apple has a sweet-but-not-too-sweet flavor.

Braeburn-A pretty new variety originally from New Zealand, this apple is crisp, sweet, juicy, and has an excellent flavor.

Calville Blanc-King Louis XIII grew this very pretty, pale yellow apple, and it is still served for dessert in fashionable restaurants in France. It has an unusual sweet spicy flavor and one of these has more vitamin C than an orange.

Chieftan-A cross between Jonathan and Delicious, but sweeter than Jonathan and a better keeper than Delicious.

Criterion-This very pretty, light yellow apple has a crisp texture, a mild flavor, and is a good keeper.

Cortland-A McIntosh cross, this large apple has deep-red stripes, a soft texture, and a tart flavor.

Empire-This is an excellent tasting and very pretty apple. It is a cross between a Red Delicious and McIntosh and is crisp and juicy.

Esopus Spitzenburg-This antique apple was Thomas Jefferson's favorite. "Spitz" is a wonderfully flavored apple that is best eaten after a month or so in storage.

Firmgold-A large red apple, it has a delicious sweet flavor and a crisp, firm texture.

Fuji-A crisp juicy apple, it is one of the world's fastest growing in popularity. It will stay crisp and juicy for months and has an excellent, sweet flavor.

Gala-This earliest of the sweet apples, Gala is quickly becoming one of the most popular apples in America. It is beautiful, with its yellow and pink skin, resembling a peach, and is crisp, spicy, and very delicious—although not for those who like their apples tart.

Golden Russett-An antique apple that is sugary, fine grained, and juicy. It has a thin russett-colored skin that is not attractive, but is an excellent keeper.

Gourmet Golden-This russet apple has an excellent complex, spicy flavor and is crisp and juicy.

Granny Smith-This sweet-tart, pretty green apple helped change the way apples are produced and marketed in America. It is an excellent tasting, late maturing apple that keeps well.

Grimes Golden-This crisp, greenish gold apple has a slight licorice sweet-tart flavor. It is available around mid-September and is not a great keeper.

Hudson's Golden Gem-This is the largest of the very good, crisp, sweet, juicy, but ugly russet apples.

Idared-For best flavor, you should store this deep red apple. It is sweet and spicy and a good keeper.

Jerseymac-This is a McIntosh cross that grows in this area.

Jonagold-A large, pretty apple, this is a cross between a Jonathan and Golden Delicious. It is a sweet and popular apple, but it is not a good keeper.

Jonalicious-This popular apple is a relative of Jonathan, but is larger, sweeter, juicier, and a better keeper.

Jonamac-This apple is a cross between a Jonathan and a McIntosh, and although not a good keeper, it has a good McIntosh flavor and can be grown well in Central Illinois (McIntosh apples don't grow well here).

Jonathan-An old apple, this is a red, sweet-tart apple that is used for cooking, eating, and cider-making.

Lady-A tiny flat apple that dates back 350 years in Europe. This apple is crisp, tart, and aromatic, and is still used in Christmas ornamentation.

Lodi-This light green summer apple has translucent flesh and is better for cooking than for eating.

Loriglo-This apple is a Jonathan mutation that is sweet and crisp and tastes like a cross between a Jonathan and a Golden Delicious.

Lura Red-This early Jonathan cross is larger and crisper than a Jonathan.

Lustre Elstar-This pretty, red-orange apple is crisp and has a sweet-tart flavor. It is best eaten two weeks after harvesting.

McIntosh-A sweet-tart apple that does not grow well in the area.

Melrose-This cross between Jonathan and Red Delicious is a better keeper than Jonathan and is especially good for baking.

Mollie's Delicious-An early, large red apple, it has a sweet aromatic flavor.

Mutsu-This wonderful, large, spicy, and juicy apple keeps well. It is sometimes marketed as a crispin apple.

Newtown Pippin-This antique apple that Benjamin Franklin enjoyed is considered a classic. Crisp and delicious, this apple is an excellent keeper that actually develops its full flavor after months of storage.

Northern Spy-Bite into this apple and be taken back to the fall bonfires of your childhood—it is that good! It has complex flavors but is not particularly attractive, and it bruises easily.

Ozark Gold-This large crisp yellow apple is sweet and juicy and a good keeper.

Paula Red-An early red apple with a sweet-tart flavor.

Pink Pearl-This pink-fleshed apple with light-green skin is a bit tart and does not keep very well.

Pitmaston Pineapple-This small russet apple is very sweet and has the distinct flavor of honey and pineapple.

Reinette Simirenko-This yellowish-green apple originated in the Ukraine. It is the apple taken into space by the Soviet cosmonauts and is a bit tart.

Rhode Island Greening-This large, green antique apple is tart and very good for cooking.

Sir Prize-A large, crisp, yellow apple, it is thin-skinned and has an excellent sweet-tart flavor.

Spartan-A cross between McIntosh and Newtown Pippin, this dark red apple is aromatic, juicy, and crisp, and a better keeper than McIntosh.

Spigold-A huge, lopsided temperamental apple, it is worth the trouble to grow it. Juicy, crisp, and having a complex spicy flavor, this is one of the truly great apples.

Sweet Sixteen-This new apple is a Northern Spy cross. It has a firm, crisp texture and a slight anise flavor.

Winesap-This crisp red apple has yellowish flesh, is juicy and tart, and is a good keeper.

Winter Banana-This large, yellow apple with a pink blush is hard, crisp, aromatic, and has a mild flavor.

York Imperial-An antique apple with a wonderfully complex flavor and crisp texture, it is an excellent keeper.

Mail-Order Shopping

Applesource
R.R. 1, Box 94
Chapin, IL 62628
(217) 245-7589

Harry and David move over. Located outside Jacksonville, Illinois, this wonderful orchard that grows more than 100 varieties of apples was recognized by *the New York Times* as one of the outstanding mail-order food businesses in the nation. Its unique catalog business allows you, or the recipient of your gift, to sample a variety of apple flavors. Applesource has a number of different boxes, containing either one or two trays of apples, from which to choose. Perhaps the most interesting are the explorer pack and the sampler pack, which contain up to 12 different varieties of apples. For the more adventurous, there is a pick-your-own (PYO) box that allows you to choose the assortment. The apples come in a heavy, nicely decorated box and are available from the end of October until January. Call or write for a copy of the Applesource catalog.

Bissinger French Confections
4742 McPherson Ave.
St. Louis, MO 63198
(314) 534-2400

Bissinger's chocolates are part of St. Louis's culinary history. Since 1926, Bissinger's has been producing exquisite chocolates that combine European skill and style with some uniquely American innovations. An elegant catalog makes it possible for people who are not fortunate enough to live near Bissinger's to order chocolates by mail. Included in the catalog is Bissinger's unique creation, the molasses caramel lollipop, made with rich molasses caramel covered in silky smooth chocolate. The catalogs contain various seasonal variations of some of Bissinger's creations. Chocolate molasses puffs, made with crunchy spun molasses; Hawaiian macadamia nuts with caramel and chocolate; heavenly hash bark; and chocolate pizza made with chocolate, pecans, and coconut are other inventive confections. Some of the more traditional European style chocolates made at Bissinger's are opera cremes, truffles, marzipan, raspberry cremes, and English toffee. Chocolate roses covered in red foil and chocolate hearts for Valentine's Day, French marshmallow chicks, chocolate Easter bunnies, gold-foil wrapped coins (*gelt*) for Hanukkah, and shaped marzipan for Christmas make welcome traditional holiday gifts. Call or write for a catalog.

Byrd's Pecans
Route 3, Box 205
Butler, MO 64730
(816) 679-5583 or (816) 925-3253

Just in time for Thanksgiving, after a hard frost or two, you can order fresh Missouri pecans for Thanksgiving pecan pies or for eating out of hand. They make welcome holiday gifts. The Byrds grow 20 or so varieties of pecans. Among the varieties are peruque, giles, hirshi, and chies. Many of the pecans are from the native trees, and the Byrds' graft different varieties to the native stock. Missouri pecans are smaller than their southern counterparts, but in a good season they can be tastier because of their higher concentration of oil. You can buy pecans shelled, cracked, or "blown," which means much of the shell is removed. They are reasonably priced. Call for information.

Funk's Grove Pure Maple Sirup
RR 1 Box 41 A
Shirley, IL 61772
(309) 874-3220 or 874-3360

When Isaac Funk came to Illinois in 1824, he made maple syrup for his family the way native Americans had taught his pioneer ancestors to. In 1891, his grandson Arthur began making it to sell. More than 100 years later, the family is still making maple syrup; sometimes a thousand gallons per year! The production of maple syrup begins in mid-February when thawing temperatures follow a hard freeze and the sap from maple trees begins to run. The earlier sap is the sweetest and needs the least cooking, so it is the lightest in color (amber) and preferrable. The darker syrup, although less delicate in flavor, is still delicious. Depending on the crop, syrup is available from the first of March until June or July and sometimes during the holiday season. You can buy the syrup mail-order, while the supply lasts, by writing or calling for a brochure.. To be sure of having some for holiday gifts, order before June 30.

Morningland Dairy
Rt. 1, Box 188B
Mountain View, MO 65548
(417) 469-3817 or (417) 469-4163

The raw milk cheese produced at Morningland Dairy is outstanding. This small family farm produces milk from a herd of 70 Holsteins that are fed in organic, chemical-free pastures. Even the fresh herbs that go into some of the cheese varieties are grown on the farm in organic beds. Their raw milk cheese, which takes more time and care to produce than cheese made from pasteurized milk, retains healthful digestive enzymes, and produces a rich creamy cheese that is simply delicious. They produce Monterry Jack, colby, and cheddar cheeses, with various herbs. The sharp cheddar is an outstanding creamy white cheese with a distinctive bite. Dill cheddar is made with a milder cheddar that has fresh, flavorful dill generously marbled throughout—an unusual treat. Chive colby is a crumbly cheese with lots of fresh chives, and garlic colby has lots of fresh garlic, yet you can still taste the mellow flavor of the cheese in both of these. You will really taste the jalapeño peppers in hot pepper Jack—so beware. Morningland Dairy cheeses are sold in many health food stores in the area, but ordering direct is far less expensive. They also have wonderful holiday gift variety packs. Call or write for a list of their cheeses and for ordering information.

John Volpi and Co.
5254 Daggett Ave.
St. Louis, MO 63110
1-800-288-3439 or (314) 772-8550

Volpi's makes wonderful Italian sausages, bacons, prosciuttos, and other cured meats. At Volpi's, they make a salami to fit every taste, from the finely grained mildly spiced Genova to the coarser, spicier "farm-style" Siciliano. Volpi is known for its classic *prosciutto crudo*, the unsmoked ham delicacy that is uncooked, but cured and ready to eat in transparently thin slices with melon or figs. Pancetta, unsmoked rolled bacon used in making authentic pasta carbonara, is another specialty at Volpi's, as is bresaola, dried and aged beef filet that is served thinly sliced with Parmesan shavings and drizzled with olive oil. For more details about Volpi's products, see the Specialty Food Shops section of this book. Volpi sells gift boxes of salamis and some other specialties, and you can order other specialty meats as well. Call for a copy of Volpi's mail-order catalog.

About the Author

Susan Taylor is the author of the local bestseller *The Guide to Good Eating in Lincoln Land and Central Illinois*. She is a member of the advisory board of the St. Louis Friends of James Beard. She is married to Stephen Spence, a blue ribbon pie baker of the Illinois State Fair. They live in St. Louis with their son Daniel.

Index by Cuisine

Index by Area

This index is organized in two parts. The first part lists places in various St. Louis neighborhoods. The second part lists places that are outside of the city in St. Louis County. (At the end of the section on St. Louis County is a listing for St. Charles.)

The area called Mid-County includes locations west of St. Louis City, east of I-270, north of Watson Rd., and south of Page Ave. Kirkwood-Webster Groves and the University City Loop have separate listings but are within Mid-County.

The area called West County includes locations west of I-270.

The area called North County includes locations from Page Ave. north.

Seasonal Products Index

Some products are available only during specific months. This index tells you when they begin to be available and where you can find them.

February: maple syrup
April: morel mushrooms, asparagus, herb plants
May: strawberries, rhubarb
June: blackberries, cherries, raspberries, blueberries
July: peaches, nectarines
August: fall raspberries, early apples, plums, pears
September: fall apples, wild mushrooms, pumpkins
October: pecans, truffles

THE GUIDE TO
Good Eating

In Lincoln Land and Central Illinois

Springfield • Champaign-Urbana
Bloomington-Normal • Decatur • Amish country

by Susan Taylor

Plan a day trip adventure!

Susan Taylor's *Guide to Good Eating in Lincoln Land and Central Illinois* leads the way to

- the best restaurants in Mr. Lincoln's hometown
- Amish whoopie pies
- maple syrup
- French cuisine in Paris, Illinois
- U-pick strawberries, blueberries, raspberries, and apples
- fresh breads, pastries, pies, and desserts
- and much, much, more

"Day trippers in the area will find invaluable Susan Taylor's *Guide to Good Eating in Lincoln Land and Central Illinois...* Take it right out of the bag or envelope and put it in the glove compartment."

> — *St. Louis Post Dispatch*

"The eater's bible"

> — *State Journal Register*

Turn to the back page of this book to order your copy.

The perfect hostess, birthday, and holiday gift

Susan Taylor's *Guide to Good Eating in St. Louis* and *Guide to Good Eating in Lincoln Land and Central Illinois* make perfect hostess gifts, birthday gifts, and holiday gifts. You can give them alone or paired with some of the wonderful foods featured inside. Shop at home and if you order 10 or more copies, you'll receive a 15% discount. And, Fifth Sin Press will pay postage on your mail order purchases. Delivery takes two to three weeks. On orders of 50 or more, an additional discount is available. For more information, write to Fifth Sin Press at the address below.

Order Form

The Guide to Good Eating in St. Louis

Send _____ copies @ $12.95 each _____

Send _____ (10 or more) copies @ $11.00 each _____

The Guide to Good Eating in Lincoln Land and Central Illinois

Send _____ copies @ $9.95 each _____

Send _____ (10 or more) copies @ $8.50 each _____

Total _____

Name_____

Address _____

City _____

State _____ ZIP_____

Mail your check or money order to: Fifth Sin Press, P.O. Box 170143, St. Louis, MO 63117